THE GREAT SECRET

THE
GREAT SECRET

or
Occultism Unveiled

by

ELIPHAS LEVI

Translated by Transcript

Studies in Hermetic Tradition : Volume III

SAMUEL WEISER INC.
734 Broadway, New York, N.Y. 10003

First published 1975

ISBN 0 7225 0293 1 (UK)
ISBN 0 87728 295 1 (USA)

Printed in Great Britain by
Redwood Burn Limited, Trowbridge & Esher

CONTENTS

FOREWORD

'Progress is a possibility for the animal: it can be broken in, tamed and trained; but it is not a possibility for the fool, because the fool thinks he has nothing to learn ... this then, at the outset, is a potent secret which is inaccessible to the majority of people – a secret which they will never guess and which it would be useless to tell them: the secret of their own stupidity.'

So says Eliphas Lévi in this the last of his works to be bequeathed to his eager public, a public which has continued to grow for more than a hundred years. What is the attraction of the writings of this unusual man who so openly scorns the mental and moral capacity of his fellow mortals? Is it that very love of mystery for mystery's sake which he so fiercely castigates in the following pages? If so, perhaps he himself was more than a little guilty of pandering to it in his earlier writings. But now he speaks openly, and yet he knows and declares that few will understand him.

However, if understanding is sometimes absent of all he is trying to tell us here, it cannot be denied that each of us with any notions at all about life and philosophy and religion will be charmed and irritated in turn as Lévi probes his pretensions. What mason will be altogether pleased to read, 'Freemasonry is only so powerful in the world because of its dread secret, so wonderfully well kept that the initiates, even those who are in the highest degrees, do not know it.'? The Catholic, perhaps, will smile, only to see in the next sentence, 'The Catholic religion keeps its hold on the masses by a secret unknown to the Pope himself.'

The old mage has got his ceremonial sword in his hand as it were and is laying about him without fear or favour. All the same, we must not suppose that he has grown miserable and misanthropic in his old age; far from it. 'Happy' he says, 'are

those who can laugh, because laughter is the attribute of man; as
the great prophet of the Renaissance, Rabelais, said, "Laughter is
forebearance, laughter is philosophy" ... the great secret of
divine omnipotence resides in an eternal smile.'

So what is Lévi trying to do in this book? In a way, one gains
the impression that, besides attempting to educate us, he is trying
to make a final synthesis of the discrepant materials which he has
culled in his search for knowledge. Three main strands can be
detected in his line of thought. As has often been mentioned, Lévi
was trained for the Roman Catholic priesthood, but either
abandoned this vocation or was debarred from pursuing it by his
superiors due to some fundamental disagreement with them. The
following pages will, perhaps, explain where this disagreement
lay. Yet it is quite clear that he did not wholly cut himself off
from Catholicism, and in fact shows that he still considers himself
to be a good Catholic (after his own fashion). 'Only the Catholics
have priests,' he asserts approvingly, 'because only they have the
altar and the sacrifice, that is to say the sum total of religion.'
And he has no room for atheism or even agnosticism: 'Religion is
no human invention, it is inevitable, that is to say providential ...
the man in the street believes in it because it is incomprehensible
to him ... I believe in it because I understand it and because I
should think it absurd not to believe in it.'

That is one of the strands, but there is another, springing from
the rationalism which helped to foment the French Revolution.
Lévi, like so many other thinkers of this and the preceding
century, had a profound respect for Science with a capital 'S'.
Nature, as we know, is hidden under many more than seven
veils, and Science keeps snatching those veils away to see what
lies beneath them; and every time she does so she changes her
mind as to what 'really' explains these appearances of reality. But
there is a touching faith abroad that Science is always right even
if Revealed Religion is sometimes wrong. Lévi fully shared this
faith, and displays it in his treatment of the Bible, of Catholicism
and of his own beloved Magical Tradition.

With him, as with the revolutionaries, reason is supreme; and,
while he is no iconoclast, whatever does not measure up to the
standards of current scientific belief must be relegated to the
status of an allegory. He believes in religion, but only because it

would be 'absurd not to believe in it.' His beliefs are based on 'reason'. Naturally, this has repercussions on his opinion of magic, as we have said. It rather seems as if the old magician had grown a little disillusioned with his former pursuits. 'Magical rituals and detailed performances in worship are all for the ignorant and superstitious', he tartly observes.

Indeed, it is evident how strongly Catholicism and rationalism modify his third main strand of thought, his magic. As far as the former influence is concerned, we can see it at work where, after giving us the formula for preparing the Ring of Solomon, he almost shrugs it aside with the words, 'An ordinary scapular, worn by a true Christian, is a more invincible talisman that the ring and the pentacle of Solomon'; and no doubt all Protestants would join Catholics in the applause when he adds, 'Jesus Christ, Son of God and Son of Man, so humble, said of Himself: "The Queen of Sheba came from the distant East to see and listen to Solomon, and a greater than Solomon is here".'

Nevertheless, there is give as well as take, and part of the respect Lévi professes for his childhood faith is due to his conviction that it is the inheritor of the authority of the occult hierarchy of the ancient world. To him, this is a commendation. The old Protestant divines of his era (notably Alexander Hislop, author of *The Two Babylons*) shared his conviction on this point, though to them it was a condemnation.

Lévi remarks somewhere, with some humour, that a sorcerer is only a thaumaturge who doesn't happen to have the Pope's approval. Even so, he is not too happy about sorcerers and others of the kind. A great deal of the theoretical side of his book is taken up with discussions of the astral currents and the importance of finding a point of balance, and he warns, 'The science of evocations is the art of magnetizing the currents in the astral light and of directing them at will ... But since the magnetic currents are fatalistic forces, one has to be a perfectly balanced centre oneself before one can control and balance them, which can hardly be said of the majority of these reckless sorcerers. They were ... often struck down in a violent flash by the imponderable fluid ...' He is arguing here from the ignorant experiments of people who dabbled with atmospheric electricity in the mistaken belief that they were contacting spirits.

But, more than this, he appears to be concerned over the general lack of sense (and sense of proportion) in those who venture into the occult world. He does not wish to be asked for yet more mystic recipes. 'I recognize,' he says, 'the relative efficacy of spells and herbs and talismans. But these are only minor devices which are linked with the lesser mysteries. I am talking to you now about the great ethical forces and not of the material instruments ... individuals who go in for ceremonial magic and stoop to consulting fortune tellers are like people who ... hope to make good their lack of true religion by multiplying their acts of devotion.' And what sceptical psychiatrist could improve on the following: 'Everything which resigns the will to mysterious forces, everything which makes other voices speak in us than the voices of conscience and reason, belongs to mental derangement ... it is we ourselves who appear to ourselves disguised as phantoms, apparitions of the dead or as demons.'?

This last dictum, like many other of Lévi's sweeping generalizations, will strike not a few readers as needing a lot of qualification, although it should by no means be ignored. In essence, it is the word of a man who appeals for a sane and natural approach. Even when commenting on the follies of the past, he can challenge the obsessions of the future, almost as if by far-sight. He makes a scathing reference to those who want to travel into the empty reaches beyond this earth, 'the splendid earth, the earth of immense oceans, the earth so full of trees and flowers ... believe me', he thunders, 'you do not need to travel far for that, the void is in your spirit and in your heart!'

You may have many books on your shelves written by men who have concentrated on being occultists; this one was written by an occultist who was not afraid to reveal himself as a man.

Transcript
Clevedon
Avon

Baron Spedalieri's* letter
to Mr Chamuel, editor of the first edition.

Marseilles,
18 August 1896

My dear Friend,

I was glad to hear that, during your stay in London, you went to see my friend Maitland, on my advice, to get access to the MSS. of various works by our master, dear Eliphas Lévi, which I had given him — among others *The Great Secret*. They are all in the Master's handwriting except the last, *The Great Secret*, for the following reason.

When, in June 1868, he had finished writing this work in his own hand for publication, he sent it to me to read and to make a copy of it. Now, it is this copy which I made with care and fidelity which I sent to Maitland. Hence you may regard it as if it were the original.

Yours fraternally,

Baron SPEDALIERI.

---

* A friend and disciple with whom Lévi had a correspondence of about a thousand letters, mainly on Qabalistic subjects, between 1861 and 1874.

INTRODUCTION

This work is the author's testament; it is the most important, and the final, treatise by him on the occult sciences.

It is divided into three books:

Book One

The Hieratic Mystery or the traditional documents of High Initiation.

Book Two

The Royal Mystery or the Art of Subduing the Powers.

Book Three

The Sacerdotal Mystery or the Art of being served by Spirits.

This treatise needs neither introduction nor preface. The author's previous works are more than sufficient to serve as both preface and introduction.

Here is the last word on occultism and it is written as clearly as it has been possible for us to write it.

Ought this volume to be published? Can it be published? We have borne these questions in mind while writing it; but we believed that we should and could write it.

If real initiates are still to be found somewhere in the world, it is for them we have written it, and to them alone belongs the right to judge us.

ELIPHAS LEVI.

September 1868.

PUBLISHER'S NOTE

Book One — The Hieratic Mystery or the traditional documents of High Initiation — referred to in Eliphas Lévi's Introduction is, in fact, *The Book of Splendours*, another posthumous work originally published in 1894, and now available in English as Volume I in our 'Studies in Hermetic Tradition' series.

BOOK TWO

The Royal Mystery
or the Art of Subduing the Powers

CHAPTER I
Magnetism

Magnetism is a force analogous to that of the ordinary magnet, and permeates the whole of nature.

Its characteristics are: attraction, repulsion and a balanced polarization.

Science takes account of celestial and mineral magnetism. Animal magnetism is exhibited daily in facts which science is unable to deny; but it regards them with mistrust, and rightly waits to admit them whenever analysis can be supplemented by an incontrovertible synthesis.

It is well known that the magnetic state produced by animal magnetism brings about an unusual type of sleep during which the soul of the magnetized individual falls under the domination of the magnetizer, with this peculiarity that the sleeper seems to leave his own life unoccupied and shows only those phenomena which belong to the universal life. He reflects the thoughts of others, sees without using his eyes, visits all places without any recognition of space, perceives forms much better than colours, foreshortens or confuses periods of time, speaks of the future as if it were past and of the past as if it were still to come, tells the magnetizer the latter's thoughts — even the secret voice of his conscience, summons into his memory the people of whom he is thinking and describes them in the greatest detail, even though the clairvoyant has never seen them, speaks the language of science like a scholar and that of the imagination like a poet, diagnoses diseases and finds the remedies for them, often imparts wise advice, suffers with those who suffer and sometimes cries bitterly beforehand when revealing the distress which has to come.

These strange but incontestable facts lead us to the necessary conclusion that there is a common life shared by all souls; or at least a common mirror for every imagination and every memory, in which it is possible for us to gaze at one another like a crowd of people standing before a glass. This reflector is the odic light of Baron Reichenbach, which we call the astral light, and is the great agency of life termed *od, ob* and *aour* by the Hebrews. The magnetism controlled by the will of the operator is Od; that of passive clairvoyance is Ob: the pythonesses of antiquity were clairvoyantes intoxicated with the passive astral light. This light is called the spirit of Python in our holy books, because in Greek mythology the serpent Python is its allegorical representative.

In its double action, it is also represented by the serpent of the caduceus: the right-hand serpent is Od, the one on the left is Ob and, in the middle, at the top of the hermetic staff, shines the golden globe which represents Aour, or light in equilibrium.

Od represents life governed by free choice, Ob represents life ruled by fate. This is why the Hebrew Law-giver said: 'Woe to those who divine by Ob, because they evoke fate, which is an offence against the providence of God and the liberty of man.'

Certainly, there is a wide difference between the serpent Python, which crawled in the mud of the deluge and was shot by the sun's arrows, and that which coils around the rod of Aesculapius, just as the tempter serpent of Eden differs from the brazen serpent which cured those who were poisoned in the desert. These two antagonistic serpents really stand for those contrary forces which may be connected but never confused. Hermes' sceptre, while keeping them apart, also reconciles them, and even unites them in a way; and this is how, under the penetrating eyes of science, harmony arises from the analogy of contraries.

Necessity and Liberty, these are the two great laws of life; and properly speaking these two laws only make one, because they are both indispensable.

Necessity without liberty would be fatal, even as liberty without its necessary curb would go insane. Privilege without obligation is folly, and obligation without privilege is slavery.

The whole secret of magnetism lies here: to rule the fatality of the *ob* by intelligence and the power of the *od* so as to create the perfect balance of *aour*.

When an unbalanced magnetizer, who has been made the slave of fate by the passions that master him, tries to operate on the light of fate, he is like a blindfold man on a blind horse, endeavouring to spur it into a gallop in a forest full of winding tracks and cliff-edges.

The fortune-tellers, the card-readers, the clairvoyants are all of them the subjects of hallucination who make their predictions by *ob*.

The glass of water in hydromancy, the tarot of Etteila, the lines in the palm, etc., produce a kind of hypnotism in the seer. Thus he regards his consultant in the reflection of his own silly desires or greedy imaginations; and because he is himself a spirit without dignity or nobility of will, he divines his client's follies and suggests to him even greater ones, which is all a part of his success so he thinks.

A card-reader who counselled honesty and upright behaviour would soon lose his clientele of kept women and hysterical old maids.

The two magnetic lights may be called one the living light and the other the dead light, one the astral fluid and the other the spectral phosphorus, one the torch of discourse and the other the smoke of dreams.

To magnetize without danger, it is essential to have within oneself the light of life, that is to say it is necessary to be wise and righteous.

The man who is a slave to his passions does not magnetize, he fascinates; but in radiating his fascination he enlarges the giddy circle around him; he multiplies his spells and saps his will power more and more. He is like a spider which wears itself out and is finally caught in its own web.

Humanity has not yet known the supreme rule of reason, even today; they mistake it for each man's personal and almost always erroneous rationalizing. However, Mr de La Palice himself would tell them that he who deceives himself is not a man of reason, for reason is just the exact opposite of our errors.

The individuals and masses who are not governed by reason are the slaves of fate; fate makes public opinion and opinion is queen of the world.

Men want to be dominated, tranquillized and led away. The major cravings seem more beautiful to them than virtues do, and those whom they call great men are often the big fools. The cynicism of Diogenes pleases them like the charlatanism of

Empedocles. There would be none they would admire so much as Ajax and Capaneus if Polyeucte had not been wilder still. Pyramus and Thisbe – who killed themselves – are the model lovers. The author of a paradox is always certain to make his name. And the world in its spite and envy has tried in vain to consign the name of Erostratus to oblivion, this name is so abnormal that it survives in their anger and imprints itself eternally on their memory!

The fools then are magnetizers or rather fascinators, and this is what makes their folly contagious. Because they have failed to measure true greatness, people get taken up with what is exotic.

Children who have not yet learnt to walk wish to be picked up and carried about.

Nobody likes wild behaviour as much as the impotent do. It is their incapacity for pleasure which makes characters like Tiberius and Messalina. The Parisian street-arab in his paradise on the boulevards would like to be a bandit and laughs uproariously on seeing Telemachus ridiculed.

Not everybody has the inclinations of drug addicts or alcoholics, but almost everyone would like to get his spirit 'high' and would be happy enough if his heart 'went on a trip'.

When Christianity imposed itself on the world by the fascination of martyrdom, a great writer of that period put the thoughts of everyone into words when he said: 'I believe because it is irrational!'

The foolishness of the Cross, as Saint Paul himself called it, was then on its invincible march. The books of the adepts were burnt, and Saint Paul at Ephesus preluded the exploits of Omar. The temples were demolished which had been the wonders of the world, and the idols which had been artistic masterpieces. People developed the taste for death and wanted to despoil their transient existence of all its ornaments so that they might withdraw from life.

A distaste for realities always goes with a love of dreams: *Quam sordet tellus dum coelum aspicio*! said a famous mystic. This means literally: How sordid the earth becomes when I look at the sky! How so; does your nurse, the earth, get dirty when your gaze loses itself in space? What is the earth then, if she is not a heavenly body? Perhaps she is dirty because she has to carry you around with her? No doubt if you were transported to the sun,

the sun would soon appear tarnished to your finicky eye! Would
the sky be a better place if it were empty? Isn't it just the point
that it is so wonderful to look at because it lights up the earth by
day and, in the night, shines with a countless multitude of earths
and suns? What, the splended earth, the earth of immense oceans,
the earth so full of trees and flowers becomes filth to you because
you want to be launched into space? Believe me, you do not need
to travel far for that: the void is in your spirit and in your heart!

It is the love of dreams which mixes so much suffering with the
dreams of love. Love, as it is given to us by nature, is a delightful
reality, but our unhealthy pride looks for something better than
nature; hence the hysterical mania of the misunderstood. The
thought of Charlotte, in Werther's head, is fatally transformed –
as is only inevitable – into the shape of a pistol bullet. The
outcome of preposterous love is suicide.

True love, natural love, is the miracle of magnetism. It is the
intertwining of the two serpents of the caduceus. Its generation
looks fated, but it is brought into being by the supreme reason
which produces it according to natural laws. It is fabled that
Tiresias incurred the wrath of Venus for separating two serpents
who were copulating, and became a hermaphrodite: which
neutralized his sexual potency; then the angry goddess struck him
again, blinding him, because he had claimed for the woman that
which was mainly the right of the man. Tiresias was a soothsayer
who prophesied by means of the dead light. His predictions, too,
announced misfortunes, and always seemed to be caused by
misfortunes. This allegory sums up the entire philosophy of
magnetism which we have just revealed.

CHAPTER II
Evil

Evil, in so far as it exists, is the affirmation of disorder. Now, in the presence of the eternal order, disorder is essentially transitory. In the presence of the absolute order, which is the will of God, disorder is only relative. Hence the absolute affirmation of disorder and evil is fundamentally a lie.

The absolute affirmation of evil is the denial of God, since God is the supreme and absolute source of good.

Evil is the denial of reason in the philosophical world. It is the denial of responsibility in the social world. It is opposition to the inviolable laws of nature in the physical world.

Suffering is not an evil, it is the consequence and nearly always the remedy of evil.

Nothing which is naturally inevitable can possibly be an evil. Winter, night and death are not evils. They are the natural transitions from one day to another day, from autumn to spring, from one life to another life.

Proudhon has said 'God is what is evil'; which is as much as to say: God is the devil, because the devil is usually taken as the spirit of evil. If we reverse the proposition, we get this paradoxical formula: The devil is God, or in other words: evil is God. But of course, in talking like this, the king of logicians whom we have quoted was not trying to designate the hypothetical personification of good under the name of God. He was dreaming of some impossible divinity imagined by men and we will agree that he was right in explaining his thought in this way, for the devil is the caricature of God, and that which we call evil is good, badly defined and poorly understood.

We should not know how to love evil for evil's sake, and

disorder for the sake of disorder. The infringement of the laws
pleases us because it seems to place us above the law. Men were
not made for the law, but the law has been made for men, to
paraphrase the saying of Jesus which the priests of his time found
so subversive and impious, a saying which human pride could
abuse so monstrously. If someone says to us that God has rights
but not responsibilities because He is stronger than we are, we
say that this is what we mean by an impious saying. He may even
dare to add that God is everything to us, but we are nothing to
Him, whereas the contrary is true. God, who is infinitely greater
than us, contracted an infinite debt in putting us into the world.
He has dug the pit of human weakness which only He can fill in.

The absurd baseness of tyranny in the ancient world has
bequeathed us the phantom of a god who is absurd and mean,
who would make an eternal miracle to force a finite being to
exist through infinite sufferings.

Let us suppose for a moment that one of us has been able to
create an ephemeral being and has said to it, without its being
able to hear it: 'My creature, worship me!' The poor little
creature scuttles about without a thought in its head. When its
day is over and it dies, a necromancer says to the man that by
pouring a drop of his blood on it he is able to resurrect the
ephemeral creature.

The man takes offence – I would do the same if I were in his
place – here is the resuscitated creature. What is the man going to
do? I will tell you what he will do, exclaims a fanatic believer.
Seeing that the creature in its former life did not have the wit to
adore him, he will light a terrible brazier and hurl the creature
into it, only regretting that he has not got the power to preserve
its life miraculously in the midst of the flames so that it will burn
eternally! – We know that everybody will say that nowhere
could such a mad fool be found as base or as wicked as that! –
Please forgive me, some of you Christians, the man in question
certainly does not exist, I am convinced of that; but there does
exist, in your imagination only I hasten to add, someone most
cruel and base. It is your idea of God, as you explain Him, and it
is of this idea that Proudhon had a thousand-fold reason for
saying: (a) God (like this) is evil.

In this sense evil would be the deceitful affirmation of an evil
god, and it is such a god who would be the devil or someone like

him. A religion which offered such a balm for the sores of humanity would poison it instead of curing it. Spirits would be brutalized and consciences would become depraved, and the propaganda made in the name of such a god could be termed the evil magnetism. The result of falsehood is injustice, and from injustice there flows the iniquity which raises anarchy in states and in individuals; disintegration and death.

A lie cannot exist without evoking in the dead light a sort of spectral verity, and all the liars in life deceive themselves first of all in taking night for day. The anarchist thinks he is free, the thief thinks he is clever, the womanizer thinks he is enjoying himself, the dictator thinks that oppression is governing. What is required to destroy evil on the earth? Something which looks very simple: the enlightenment of the dolts and the vicious. But here all goodwill fails and all efforts founder; the vicious and the dolts have no wish to be enlightened. We have come up against that secret perversity which seems to be the root of the trouble, the relish for disorder and the attachment to error. It is our opinion that this perversity is not really something which is freely accepted and desired, but is nothing else than the poisoning of the will by the deleterious force of error.

The air we breath consists, as you know, of oxygen and nitrogen. The oxygen corresponds to the light of life and the nitrogen to the light of death. A man who was plunged into nitrogen would be unable to breathe or live; in the same way, a man who has been asphyxiated by the spectral light is no longer able to act of his own free will. It is not in the atmosphere that the great phenomenon of light takes place, it is in eyes which have been formed to see. One day, a philosopher of the positivist school, Mr Littré if I remember correctly, declared that infinity is nothing more than an endless night punctuated here and there by one or two stars. This is true, someone will say, for our eyes, which have not been made to perceive any other radiance than the light of the sun. But does not the very idea of this light appear to us when dreaming, while the earth is shrouded in night and our eyes are shut? What is the day belonging to souls? How does one see by means of thought? Would the night of our eyes exist for eyes which were constructed in some other way? And if our eyes were non-existent, would we have any awareness of the night? There are neither stars nor sun to the blind; and if we blindfold our eyes we become blind voluntarily. The perversity of the senses just like that of the faculties of the soul results from an accident or from some first offence against the laws of nature; it then becomes necessary and has the appearance of being fated. What is to be done with the blind? – They must be taken by the hand and led. – But what if they do not want to be led? – Guard-rails will have to be erected. – But suppose they knock them down? – In that case they are not simply blind, but dangerous lunatics and the best thing to do is to let them perish if they cannot be locked up.

Edgar Allan Poe tells the amusing story of an asylum where the inmates had managed to lay hands on the attendants and keepers and had locked them in their own padded cells after making them look like wild beasts. There they are, celebrating their victory in their doctor's rooms, drinking the infirmary's wine and congratulating each other on having made such splendid recoveries. While they are carousing, their prisoners break their chains and rush them with flailing batons. They have been infuriated by the poor madmen and avenge themselves after a fashion by senseless ill-usage.

Here we have the story of modern revolutions. The feeble-minded, triumphing by sheer weight of numbers, in other words the so-called masses, imprison the wise men and make out that the latter are no better than wild beasts. Soon the prisons fall into disrepair and break down, and the wise of today, by their sufferings, escape howling and spreading terror all round. An attempt was made to impose a false god on people, and they bawl that there is no God at all. Then the apathetic, who have grown bold from fear, form a coalition to quell these frantic half-wits and inaugurate the rule of the imbeciles. We have already seen this happen.

Up to what point men are responsible for the swings and agonies which produce so many crimes, would puzzle a thinker to say. Marat is execrated and Pius V is canonized.

It is true that the awful Ghislieri did not guillotine his opponents – he burnt them to death. Pius V was a severe man and a convinced Catholic. Marat took impartiality to the point of misery.

Both of them believed in what they were doing, but they were homicidal fools even if they were not homicidal maniacs.

Now, when some criminal folly obtains the complicity of the people it almost becomes a terrible right, and when the mob, who have not been undeceived but led astray in some other fashion, disown and abandon their hero, the loser becomes at one and the same time both scapegoat and martyr. The death of Robespierre is as fine as that of Louis XVI.

I genuinely admire that frightful inquisitor who, when assassinated by the Albigenses, wrote on the ground with his blood before he died: *Credo in unum Deum*! (I believe in One God).

Is war an evil? Yes, of course it is, because it is horrible. But is it an absolute evil? — War is the travail at the birth of nations and civilizations. Who is responsible for war? Are men? No, for they are its victims. Who then? — No one would be rash enough to say Providence; unless perhaps Count Joseph de Maistre, with his theories of why the priests have always consecrated the sword and how there has always been a mystical air associated with the bloody office of the executioner. Evil is the shadow, the foil of good. Pushing this argument too far would imply that it is negative good. Evil then, is the resistance which confirms the effort of good, and so that is why Jesus Christ was not afraid to say: 'It must needs be that scandals should come!'

There are monsters in nature, just as there are typographical faults in a fine book. What does this show? It shows that both nature and the press are blind instruments directed by intelligence; but, you will say to me, a good case overseer will correct his proofs. Yes indeed, and in nature this is the purpose of progress.

God, if I may be allowed the comparison, is like the head of the printing works and man is His overseer in the composing room.

The priests have always preached that scourages are caused by human sins, and they are right, because science has been given to man to foresee and prevent scourges. If, as is claimed, cholera arises from the corpses piled up at the mouths of the Ganges, if famine comes of cornering food, if plague is caused by dirtiness, if war is so often caused by the stupid pride of kings and the unruliness of peoples, is it not really the wickedness — or rather the silliness — of men which is the cause of scourges?

There is an expression that 'ideas are in the air', and one may truthfully add that vices are there too. All corruption produces putrefaction and every putrefaction has its own identifiable stench. The atmosphere which envelopes the sick is unhealthy, and the moral plague has its own atmosphere which is far more contagious. An honest heart feels at ease in the company of good men, but it is oppressed, it suffers, it is stifled when surrounded by the vicious.

CHAPTER III
Joint Liability in Evil

In his book on the perpetual motion of souls, the Grand Rabbi Isaac Loriah says that it is necessary to take special care in using the hour preceding sleep. In fact, the soul loses its individual life for a time during sleep to immerse itself in the universal light which, as we have said, appears as two opposite currents. The sleeping entity either yields to the embraces of the serpent of Aesculapius, the vital and regenerating serpent, or lies back in the poisoned coils of the hideous Python. To sleep is to bathe in the light of life or in the phosphorescent glow of death. He who goes to sleep with thoughts of justice steeps himself in the merits of the just, but he who prepares for sleep with hatred or lies filling his mind wallows in the dead sea or soaks up the infection of the wicked.

Night is like winter time which incubates and prepares the seeds. If we have sown tares we shall not harvest wheat. He who settles down to sleep in a spirit of irreverence will not wake up in the presence of the divine blessing. It is said that night brings counsel. Undoubtedly. Good counsel to the just, and baneful impulses to the unjust. These are the teachings of Rabbi Isaac Loriah.*

We do not know how far one ought to admit this reciprocal influence between beings plunged in sleep and controlled in some fashion by involuntary attractions, so that the good improve the good, and the wicked make those who are like them worse still. It would be more comforting to think that the good nature of the just shines on the wicked to calm them down, and that the restiveness of the wicked cannot affect the soul of the just. What is certain, is that evil thoughts disturb the sleep and make it

* Isaac Loriah *Traité des Révolutions des Ames* (P. Chacornac, 1905).

unwholesome in consequence, and that a good conscience does wonders in refreshing and resting the blood during sleep.

At the same time it is highly probable that the magnetic radiation which has been fixed during the day by the habits and the will, does not stop during the night. This is proved by the fact that our dreams are where we often act out our most secret desires. 'Only he,' says St Augustine 'has truly attained the virtue of chastity who imposes modesty even on his dreams.'

All the stars are magnetic, and all the celestial magnets act and react on one another in the planetary systems, in the universes and throughout infinity! The same holds good for the beings living on the earth.

The nature and force of the magnets is determined by the reciprocal influence of their forms on the force and of the force on their forms. It is necessary to examine and meditate on this with serious attention.

That beauty which is the harmony of forms is always associated with a great power of attraction; but there are doubtful and debatable beauties.

There are conventional beauties in line with certain tastes and certain passions. It was discovered at the court of Louis XV that the Venus de Milo had a large waist and big feet. In the East, the sultan's concubines are fat and, in the kingdom of Siam women are bought by weight.

Men are prepared to perpetrate follies for the beauty which subjugates them, whether that beauty is real or imaginary. So it is forms then which intoxicate us and exercise the empire of fatal forces over our better judgement. When our tastes are depraved we are smitten with certain imaginary beauties which are really eyesores. When the Romans became decadent they fell in love with the low brow and frog eyes of Messalina. Down here everyone makes his own kind of paradise. But this is where justice comes in: the paradise of depraved creatures is always and inevitably a hell.

It is the intentions of the will which decide the value of deeds, because it is the will which fixes the goal one sets for oneself, and it is always the goal desired and attained which governs the character of one's works. It is according to our works that God will judge us, as the Evangelist says, and not according to our deeds. Our deeds prepare, begin, carry on and finish our works.

They are good when the work is good, and bad when it is bad. We have no wish to say that the end justifies the means, only that a worthy end necessitates worthy means and imparts some merit to actions of the most indifferent sort.

You do or get done the thing of which you approve because you encourage it. If your rule of conduct is false, if your aims are iniquitous, all those who think like you do behave as you would behave if you were them; and when they succeed, you think they have done well. If your actions seem to be those of a good man, while all the time your intentions are those of a scoundrel, your actions will become wicked. The prayers of the hypocrite are more impious than the blasphemies of the miscreant. To sum up, everything which promotes injustice is unjust; everything one does for justice is just and good.

We have already said that human beings are magnets which act one on another. This magnetism which is natural at first, but is afterwards settled in a mode determined by the habits of the will, groups mankind in phalanges and sets far more perhaps than Fourier imagined. Anyway, it is true to say with him that the attractions are proportional to the destinies; but he went wrong when he failed to differentiate between inevitable attractions and artificial attractions. He also believed that criminals are those who are misunderstood by society, whereas on the contrary it is they who do not understand society and have no intention of understanding it. What would he have done in his phalanstery with people whose attraction, proportional to their destiny according to him, had disrupted and tended to disintegrate the phalanstery?

In our book entitled *The Science of Spirits*, we have set down the traditional qabalistic classification of good and evil spirits. Superficial readers may have asked: why these names rather than others? What spirit descending from heaven, or what soul climbing back out of the abyss, has been able to reveal these hierarchical secrets of the other world? All this is nothing but the height of fantasy. But in saying so, these readers would have been deceived. This classification is not arbitrary, and if we postulate the existence of such and such spirits in the other world it is because they most certainly do exist there. Anarchy, presumption, obscurantism, fraud, hatred and unfairness are set against wise conduct, authority, intelligence, honour, kindness and justice. The Hebrew names Kether, Chokmah, Binah; the names Thamiel, Chaigidel, Satariel, etc., opposed to the names Hajoth Haccadosh, Ophanim, Aralim, etc., signify nothing else.

The same is true of all the important words and all the obscure terms of any dogma, ancient or modern; in the last analysis they enshrine the principles of eternal and incorruptible reason. It is evident, yes certain, that the masses are not yet ripe for the reign of reason and that the biggest fools or the biggest knaves among them mislead them time and again with blind creeds. Folly for folly, I can find more genuine socialism in Loyola than I can in Proudhon.

Proudhon affirms that atheism is an article of faith, the worst of all, it is true, which is why he has adopted it. He affirms that God is bad, that the social order is anarchy, that property is theft! What society is possible on such principles?

The Society of Jesus is established on the opposite principles, call them opposite errors if you like, and for centuries now it has held its own and is still strong enough to hold its own against the partisans of anarchy for years to come.

It is not perfectly balanced, it is true, but it still knows how to throw heavier weights on the scales than those of our friend Proudhon.

Men are more united in evil than they imagine. Proudhon made Veuillot what he was. Those who lit the faggots at Constance will have to answer before God for the massacres of Jean Ziska. The Protestants are responsible for the massacre of Saint Bartholomew's Day because they cut the throats of the Catholics. Perhaps in reality it is Marat who has killed Robespierre, just as it is Charlotte Corday who caused her friends the Girondins to be executed. Madame Dubarry, dragged to the national abattoire like a slaughterhouse animal lowing and unwilling, no doubt had no thought that she must pay the penalty for the tortures under Louis XVI. For often our greatest crimes are those we do not realize.

When Marat said that one task or humanity is to let a little blood to prevent a bigger haemorrhage still, from whom do you think he borrowed this maxim? – From the mild and pious Fénelon.

Not long ago the previously unpublished letters of Madame Elisabeth were printed and, in one of these letters, the angelic princess declares that all is lost unless the king has the courage to cut off three heads. Whose? She does not say, perhaps those of Philippe d'Orléans, of La Fayette and of Mirabeau! A prince of her own family, a worthy man and a great man. Little does it matter; the gentle princess would like three heads. Later on Marat was asking for three hundred thousand; between the angel and the demon there is only a difference of a few zeros.

CHAPTER IV
The Double Chain

The movement of the serpents around the caduceus indicates the formation of a chain.

This chain exists in two forms: the straight form and the circular form. Starting from the same centre it intersects innumerable circumferences by innumerable radii. The straight chain is the chain of transmission. The circular chain is the chain of participation, of diffusion, of communion, of religion. In this manner is formed that wheel, made up of several wheels turning one within another, which flashes on us from the vision of Ezekiel. The chain of transmission introduces solidarity between successive generations.

The central point is white on one side and black on the other.

The black serpent is fastened to the black side, and the white serpent is fastened to the white side. The central point represents original free will, and on its black side begins the original sin.

The current of fate starts from the black side, whereas choice of movement is attached to the white side. The central point may be allegorically represented by the moon, and the two forces by two women, one of them white and the other black.

The black woman is fallen Eve, she is the passive form, the infernal Hecate who bears the lunar crescent on her forehead. The white woman is Maia or Maria who treads under foot both the crescent moon and the head of the black serpent.

It is impossible to express the matter more clearly, because we have rested our hand on the cradle of all the dogmas. They have reverted to infancy before our very eyes, and we are wary lest we should harm them.

The doctrine of original sin, in whatever fashion it may be interpreted, assumes the pre-existence of our souls, if not in their own special life, at least in the universal life.

Now, if one can sin without knowing it in the universal life, one must needs be saved in the same way; but this is a great mystery.   .

The straight chain, the spoke of the wheel, the chain of transmission, produces solidarity between the generations, ensuring that the fathers are punished in their children so that, by the sufferings of the children the fathers stand a chance of being saved.

The Scriptures tell us that Christ descended into Hell and, having broken the iron locks and the doors of brass, ascended into Heaven leading captivity captive.

And the Universal Life cried out: Hosanna! For He has removed the sting of Death!

What is meant by all this? Dare one explain it? Will you be able to guess or understand it?

The ancient hierophants of Greece had another way of representing the two forces illustrated by the two serpents; this was as two children struggling with one another while holding a globe between their feet and knees.

The two children are Eros and Anteros, Cupid and Hermes, foolish love and wise love; and their everlasting fight keeps the world in equilibrium.

If one does not agree that we may have had some personal existence before our birth on earth, original sin will have to be seen as a voluntary depravity of human magnetism in our first parents, who would have broken the equilibrium of the chain by allowing a deadly predominance to the black serpent, that is to say, the astral current of the dead life; and we are suffering the consequences like children who are born with rickets owning to their parents' vices; feeling the penalty of misdoings which they did not commit themselves.

The extreme sufferings of Jesus and the martyrs, the excessive penances of the saints, were intended as a counterpoise to this lack of equilibrium; so irreparable, it must be added, that the world will one day be burnt up. Grace would be typified by the dove and the lamb; the astral current of life charged with the merits of the Redeemer or the saints.

The Devil or Tempter would be the astral current of death; the black serpent stained with all the crimes of men, scaled with their evil thoughts, loaded with the poison of their sinful desires; in other words THE MAGNETISM OF EVIL.

Now then, between good and evil an unending conflict is waged. They are irreconcilable for ever. So evil is always damned, always condemned to the torments which go with disorder, and yet, from our childhood it never ceases to entice us and to attract us to its side. Everything which mystical poetry teaches us about king Satan is perfectly explained in terms of this appalling magnetism which is so much the more terrible as it is more fatal; yet need not be feared so much by virtue, which it cannot overtake and which, by God's grace will surely resist it.

CHAPTER V
The Outer Darkness

We have stated that the phenomenon of physical light manifests and takes place solely in the eyes which see it. That is to say that visibility has no existence for us without the faculty of vision.

The same is true of the intellectual light, it only exists for those intelligences which are capable of seeing it. It is that inner light for lack of which there is nothing but the outer darkness where, according to the words of Christ, there is and will always be wailing and gnashing of teeth.

The enemies of the truth resemble child delinquents, overturning and putting out all the lamps, because they can scream and cry in the dark more easily.

Truth is so inseparably bound up with what is good that every evil deed freely consented to and done without a twinge of conscience, extinguishes the light of our soul and casts us out into the outer darkness.

This is the essence of mortal sin. The sinner is represented in the ancient fable by Oedipus who, having killed his father and violated his mother, ended by putting out his own eyes.

Knowledge is the father of human intelligence, and faith is its mother.

There were two trees in the Garden of Eden, the tree of knowledge and the tree of life.

It is knowledge which should and which can fertilize faith; otherwise she exhausts herself with monstrous abortions and gives birth to nothing but phantoms.

It is faith which ought to be the recompense of knowledge and the object for which he strives, without her he ends by doubting himself, becomes greatly discouraged and very soon despairing.

Thus the believers, on the one hand, who despise science and misunderstand nature, and the scientists, on the other hand, who insult, reject and would like to destroy faith, are both of them the enemies of the light and dash out to contend with one another in the outer darkness where Proudhon and ·Veuillot raise their voices turn and turn about, in a way which sounds worse than tears, and go on to grind their teeth.

True faith cannot possibly come into conflict with true science. Also, every explanation of dogma which science demonstrates as false ought to be rejected by faith.

We are no longer living in the days when it is the fashion to say: I believe it because it is beyond reason. We must say nowadays: I believe because it would be unreasonable not to do so; *Credo quia absurdum non credere.*

Science and faith are not two engines of war set on a collision course: they are the two columns destined to support the pediment of the temple of peace. It is necessary to clean the gold of the sanctuary so often tarnished by the grime of priestcraft.

Christ said: 'The words of the doctrine are spirit and life, the letter counts for nothing.' He also said: 'Judge not that ye be not judged, for with whatsoever judgment ye judge ye shall be judged, and as ye measure so shall it be meted out unto you.' What a splendid eulogy on the wisdom of reasonable doubt! And what a proclamation of liberty of conscience! In fact, one thing will be clear to anyone who likes to listen to sound sense; it is that if there is a strict law applicable to all, without the keeping of which it is impossible to be saved, this law will have to be promulgated in such a way as to leave no-one in doubt of its enactment. In such a matter, the possibility of doubt is a formal negation; and if a single man could be left in ignorance of such a law, the law would not be divine.

There are no two ways of being a decent man; and does religion matter less than probity? Certainly not, and this is why there has never been anything but one religion in the world. The schisms are only appearances. It is the fanaticism of the ignorant who mutually condemn each other which has always been irreligious and horrible.

The true religion is the universal religion; which is why Catholicism has adopted the only name which indicates the truth. Furthermore, this religion maintains orthodoxy in doctrine, the hierarchy of the powers, the efficacy of worship and the genuine magic of ceremonies. In other words it is typical and normal religion, the mother religion to which the Mosaic traditions and the ancient oracles of Hermes rightly belong. In upholding this in the face of the Pope himself if necessary, we shall be more catholic than the Pope and more protestant than Luther when occasion demands.

True religion is the inner light above all else, and religious forms so often multiply and shine with the spectral phosphorescence which is in the outer darkness; but it is necessary to respect the form even with those souls who do not understand the spirit. Science cannot and must not make reprisals against ignorance.

Fanaticism does not know why faith is reasonable, and reason, while recognizing that religion is essential, has a perfect understanding of how and why superstition is wrong.

The whole Christian and Catholic religion is based on the doctrine of grace, that is to say of free gift. Freely you have received, freely give, says Saint Paul. Religion is essentially a charitable institution. The Church is a house of refuge for the outcasts of philosophy. We may leave her, but we must never attack her. The poor who make do without public assistance have not earned themselves the right to sneer at it. The man who lives uprightly without religion deprives himself of tremendous assistance, but he is not setting himself against God. Free gifts are not replaced by punishments if we refuse them, and God is not a usurer who makes men pay interest on what they have not borrowed. Men need religion, but religion does not need men. Those who do not acknowledge the law, says Saint Paul, will be judged without the law. Now, he is not speaking here of the natural law, but of the religious law or, to be more precise, of the sacerdotal ordinances.

Beyond these truths so benign and pure, there is nothing else but that outer darkness where those are wailing whom a misconstrued religion cannot console, and where the sectarians who take hate for love are gnashing their teeth at one another.

One day, Saint Theresa had a tremendous vision. It seemed to her that she was in Hell and that she was immured within huge walls which were closing in around her in the vain attempt to suffocate her. These walls were quite tangible and have often led us to muse on that menacing saying of Christ about 'the outer darkness'. Imagine a soul which, through hatred of the light, has blinded itself like Oedipus; it has resisted all the charms of life and has always repulsed life as it has repulsed light. Here it is, hurled beyond the influence of the worlds and the brightness of the suns. It is alone in the immense darkness, where it must dwell by itself and with the other wilfully blind who resemble it, for ever. It is fixed in the shadow and suffers an eternal suffocation in the night. It seems to it that everything has been destroyed except its own sufferings, which could fill infinity.

What misery! To have had the capacity for understanding and to have persisted in the idiocy of a senseless creed! To have been able to love and to have allowed the heart to wither! Oh, just for an hour or even one minute of the most imperfect pleasures or the most fleeting loves! Just a little air! A little sun! or even the moonlight and dancing on the green! A drop of life or less than a drop — a tear! And an implacable eternity replies: What is this talk of tears: you cannot even cry! Tears are the dew of life and the oozing of the sap of love; you have exiled yourself in your egotism and have walled yourself up in death.

Ah! you wanted to be holier than God! Ah! you spat in the face of your mother, the chaste and divine nature! Ah! you have spoken ill of science, of intelligence and progress! Ah, you believed that eternal life meant looking like a corpse and dessicating oneself like a mummy! Now you are what you have made yourself, rejoice in the eternity which you have chosen — in peace! But no, you poor people, those you call the sinners and the damned are coming to save you. We shall intensify the light, we shall pierce your wall, we shall tear you from your inertia. A swarm of cupids, or if you prefer, a legion of angels (they are made in the same way) shall spiral around you and drag you forth in festoons of flowers; and you shall protest in vain, like Mephistopheles in that marvellous philosophical drama by Goethe. In spite of yourselves, your restrictions and your pale faces, you will revive, you will love, you will know, you will see, and you will come to dance the infernal jig of Faust with us on the rubble of the last cloister!

Happy in the time of Jesus were those who wept! Happy, now, are those who can laugh, *because laughter is the attribute of man*, as the great prophet of the Renaissance, Rabelais, said. Laughter is forbearance; laughter is philosophy. The heavens clear when they laugh, and the great secret of divine omnipotence resides in an eternal smile!

CHAPTER VI
The Great Secret

Wisdom, morality, virtue: these are respectable words, but also vague ones; and they have been the subjects of dispute for centuries without there being any agreement on them!

I wish to be wise, but shall I remain certain of my wisdom as long as I suspect that fools are happier or even more jolly than I am?

Morality is essential; but we are all a little like children, and moralizing makes us yawn. This is because people try to stuff us with stupid morals which are not adapted to our nature. People lecture us on things which have nothing to do with us, and our minds wander.

Virtue is a fine thing: its name really means force, power. The world is upheld by the virtue of God. But in what does virtue consist for us? Is it a virtue to fast so as to weaken the head and emaciate the face? Shall we say that virtue is the simplicity of the worthy man who lets himself be robbed by thieves? Is abstinence for the sake of avoiding abuse a virtue? What would you think of a man who refused to walk for fear of breaking a leg? Whichever way you look at it, virtue is opposed to slackness, lethargy and impotence.

Virtue presupposes action; for the reason why is is usually contrasted with our passions is to make it clear that it is never something passive.

Not only is virtue strength, it is the governing reason behind strength. It is the equilibrant of life.

The great secret of virtue, virtuality and life, whether temporal or eternal, may be formulated thus:

The art of balancing forces so as to keep movement in equilibrium.

The equilibrium we are looking for is not that which produces immobility, but that which regulates movement. For immobility is death, and movement is life.

This motive equilibrium is that of nature itself. Nature, by balancing the decisive forces, produces the physical illness or even the apparent destruction of the poorly balanced man. Mankind rids itself of natural ills by knowing how to escape from the fatal action of the forces through an intelligent use of its liberty. We employ the word fatal here because the unforeseen and misunderstood forces look like necessary fate to the ill-balanced man.

Nature has provided for the conservation of the animals by endowing them with instinct, but she has arranged everything so that the improvident man will perish.

The animals live, so to speak, of their own accord and without effort. Man alone has to learn the way to live. Now the science of life is the science of moral balance.

The basis of this balance is to reconcile knowledge and religion, reason and feeling, energy and gentleness.

Truly invincible strength is strength without violence. Violent men are weak and shortsighted men whose efforts always come back on themselves.

Violent affection resembles hatred, and is close kin to aversion.

Violent anger ensures that one gives oneself up to one's enemies blindly. Homer's heroes, when attacking one another, made a point of hurling mutual insults in an attempt to rouse each other's fury, knowing full well that, in all probability, the more infuriated of the two would be conquered.

Fiery-tempered Achilles was foredoomed to perish miserably. He was the proudest and the bravest of the Greeks and brought nothing but disasters upon the heads of his compatriots.

What took Troy was the prudence and patience of Odysseus, who always held himself in check and never struck unless he was certain of success. Achilles stands for passion, and Odysseus stands for virtue, and we need to bear this in mind before we can understand the high philosophical and moral significance of the Homeric poems.

Without doubt, the author of these poems was an initiate of the first order, and the great secret of practical High Magic is all there in the Odyssey.

The great secret of magic, the unique and incommunicable Arcana, has for its purpose the placing of supernatural power at the service of the human will in some way.

To attain such an achievement it is necessary to KNOW what has to be done, to WILL what is required, to DARE what must be attempted and to KEEP SILENT with discernment.

Homer's Odysseus had to contend with the gods, the elements, the cyclops, the sirens, Circe, etc. ... that is to say with all the difficulties and dangers of life.

His palace is invaded, his wife is pestered, his goods are plundered, his death is resolved on, he loses his comrades, his ships are sunk; at last, he alone is left to fight it out against the night and the sea. And single-handed he sways the gods, he escapes from the sea, he blinds the cyclops, he cheats the sirens, he masters Circe, he re-takes his palace, he rescues his wife, he slays those who were plotting his death; because he *willed* to see Ithaca and Penelope again, because he always *knew* how to extricate himself from danger, because he *dared* what had to be done and because he always *kept silent* when it was not expedient to speak.

But those who are fond of fairy-tales will say, with some disappointment, this isn't magic at all. Aren't there any talismans, or herbs or roots with which one can work marvels? Aren't there any mysterious spells which will open locked doors and conjure up spirits? Talk to us about this, and leave your commentary on the Odyssey for another occasion.

You know, my children, for there is no doubt that I have to reply to children, you know, if you have read my previous works, that I recognize the relative efficacy of spells and herbs and talismans. But these are only minor devices which are linked with the lesser mysteries. I am talking to you now about the great ethical forces and not of the material instruments. Spells belong to initiation rites, talismans are magnetic auxiliaries, roots and herbs fall within the province of occult medicine, and Homer himself did not disdain them. Moly, the lotus and nepenthe have their place in his poems, but they are there as incidental ornaments. Circe's cup could not affect Odysseus, who recognized its baleful results and knew how to avoid drinking it. The initiate into the high science of the mages has nothing to fear from sorcerers.

Those individuals who go in for ceremonial magic and stoop to consulting fortune-tellers are like the people who intend or hope to make good their lack of true religion by multiplying their acts of devotion. It would be a waste of time trying to satisfy them with sage advice.

You are all of you hiding a secret which is very easily guessed, and it is this: I have a passion which reason condemns and I prefer it to reason; that is why I consult an irrational oracle, because it tells me to keep hoping, helps me to trick my conscience, and lulls my heart into a feeling of security.

Folk of this sort, then, go to drink from a deceitful spring which, far from quenching their thirst, intensifies it. The charlatan mutters dark oracles, where one finds whatever one wants to find and departs knowing as little as ever. One returns on the morrow, and on the day after that, and in fact one always returns; which is how those who read the cards make their fortunes.

The Basilidian gnostics said that Sophia, the natural wisdom of man, fell in love with herself, as Narcissus did in the fable, looked away from her primary source and sprang out of that circle traced by the divine light which they called the pleroma. All alone in the darkness, she committed sacrileges in order to give birth to the light; and lost her blood like the woman with the issue of blood in the Gospel, giving rise to horrible monsters. The most dangerous of all follies is perverted wisdom.

Perverted hearts poison the whole of nature. The splendour of a beautiful day is no more to them than a garish distraction, and all the joys of life, which are dead for these dead souls, rise up in front of them to curse them, saying like the ghosts to Richard III: 'Despair and die.' Enthusiasm for noble causes makes them smirk and, as if they were requiting an insult, they throw the insolent sneers of Sténio and Rollon at love and beauty. It is no use dropping one's arms and blaming fate; what has to be done is to fight it and conquer. Those who succumb in this battle are those who do not know how to win or do not want to do so. Not knowing is some excuse, but it is no justification when the opportunity to learn is there. 'Father, forgive them, for they know not what they do,' said Christ when dying. If a lack of knowledge were permissible, the Saviour's prayer would have been without justice, and His Father would have had nothing to pardon.

When one does not know, one should *will* to learn. To the extent that one does not *know* it is foolhardy to *dare*, but it is always well to *keep silent*.

CHAPTER VII
The Creating and Transforming Power

The will is the practical realizer: we can do everything which we believe is a reasonable project.

In his own sphere of action, man is the image of the all-powerful God; he is able both to create and to transform.

His first task is to exercise this power on himself. When he enters the world, his faculties are a chaos, the darkness of his intellect covers the abyss of his heart, and his spirit is poised in uncertainty as if it were swept here and there by the waves.

He has been endowed with reason, but this reason is still passive and it is up to him to rouse it into activity; to let his face shine in the midst of the waves and cry: let there be light!

He develops a rational mind, he develops a conscience, he develops a heart. The divine law will express just what he has been doing, and the whole of nature will become for him exactly what he would like it to be.

Eternity will enter and remain in his memory. He will say to spirit: be matter, and to matter: be spirit, and spirit and matter will obey him!

All substance is modified by action, all action is controlled by spirit, all spirit is controlled conformably to the will, and all will is decided by some reason.

The reality of things is in their reason for existing, and this reason for things is the principle of that which is.

There is nothing other than force and matter, say the atheists.

They might just as well declare that books are nothing more than paper and ink.

Matter is the adjunct of the spirit; without the spirit it would have no reason to exist, and it would not exist.

Matter is changed into spirit by the agency of our senses, and this transformation, perceptible only to our souls, is the thing we call pleasure.

Pleasure is the sensation of a divine action. Letting it thrive creates life and transforms dead compounds into living substances in the most marvellous manner.

Why does nature draw the two sexes together with so much rapture and intoxication? Because she invites them to the great work *par excellence*, the work of eternal fruitfulness.

What talk is that about the joys of the flesh? The flesh has neither griefs nor joys: it is but a passive instrument. Our nerves are the violin strings with which nature makes us hear and feel the music of sensual delight; and all the joys of life, even those which are most spoilt, are the exclusive share of the soul.

What is beauty, if not the imprint of spirit on matter? Does the body of the Venus de Milo need to be flesh to enchant our eyes and inflame our thoughts? Woman's beauty is the hymn of motherhood; the soft and delicate shape of her breasts never fails to remind us of the first thirst of our lips; we should like to repay them with eternal kisses for the sweet drink they gave us. Does this mean that we are in love with the flesh? Despoil them of their adorable poetry and what inspiration could one find in these 'rubber pillows' filled with glands under a skin now brown and now pink and white? And whatever would become of our most charming emotions if the hand of the lover, no longer trembling, had to arm itself with the magnifying glass of the physician or the scalpel of the anatomist?

Apuleus, in a clever fable, recounts how a blundering experimenter, having seduced the maidservant of a female magician, got from her an ointment which had been prepared by her mistress. He attempted to change himself into a bird, but only succeeded in transforming himself into an ass. He was told that to recover his original form, all that he needed to do was to feed on some roses, and his first thought was how easy this would be. However, he soon found out that roses were not made for the benefit of donkeys. Whenever he tried to get near a rose-bush, he was driven off with cudgel blows. He suffered a thousand misfortunes, and was only saved at last by the direct intervention of the gods.

Some people have suspected that Apuleus was a Christian, and have tried to read into this legend of the Ass a sly dig at the mysteries of Christianity. Eager to mount upward into the heavens, so they say, the Christians disowned science and fell under the yoke of that blind faith which caused them to be accused, in the first centuries, of worshipping the head of an ass.

Having become enslaved to a fatal asceticism, they were no longer able to get close to those natural beauties which are typified by roses. Pleasure, beauty, even nature and life themselves were anathematized by these ungracious and ignorant guides, who drove from their presence the poor ass of Bethlehem. It is at this period that the Middle Ages dreamt of 'The Romance of The Rose'. It is then that the Initiates into the sciences of antiquity, anxious to regain the rose without renouncing the cross, put the two together and adopted the name Rosae Crucis (or Rosicrucian) so that the rose was still the cross and the cross could immortalize the rose.

The only true pleasure, true beauty and genuine love belongs to the wise; who are actually the creators of their own happiness. When they abstain from something it is to learn how to use it properly and, when they deprive themselves, it is to gain some delight in exchange.

What misery is more to be pitied than that of the soul, and how well-entitled to lament are those who have impoverished their hearts! Compare the poverty of Homer with the wealth of Trimalcion, and say which of them is the poor wretch. What is the good of possessions if they pervert us, seeing that they are never really ours but will inevitably be lost or left to others? What purpose do they serve if they are not the instruments of wisdom in our hands? Are they for ministering to the wants of animal life, to brutalize us with satiety and loathing: is that the aim of our existence? Is that a positive way of life? Surely, it is the falsest and most depraved of ideals? Anyone who employs his soul about the business of fattening his carcase is already playing a fool's game; but to wear out both body and soul for the privilege of leaving behind a fortune to be squandered by a young idiot, who will surrender it into the lap of the first loose woman who gets her hands on him, is that not the height of lunacy? Yet such are the actions of responsible men who look on philosophers and poets as dreamers.

What I prize, said Curius, is not to own great wealth but to have those who do at my command, and Saint Vincent de Paul, probably without thinking of Curius's maxim, revealed its full grandeur in the service of charity. What monarch would ever have been able to found so many alms-houses or to endow so many places of refuge for the homeless? What Rothschild would have managed to find enough millions for all that? The poor priest, Vincent de Paul, was determined to do it; he spoke and riches obeyed him.

His secret lay in possessing the power which creates and transforms, a persevering will and a wise application of the most sacred laws of nature. Learn to will what God wishes, and everything you want will certainly happen.

You must also understand that contraries materialize through contraries: greed is always poor, unselfishness is always rich.

Pride provokes scorn, modesty wins praise, over-indulgence in sex kills pleasure, moderation refines and renews sensual enjoyment. You will get, every time, the opposite of whatever you want to have unfairly, and you will be repaid a hundred times over for anything you sacrifice to justice. So, if you wish to reap on the left hand, sow on the right hand; and meditate on this piece of advice, which looks like a paradox and will give you a hint of one of the greatest secrets of occult philosophy.

If you desire to attract, make a vacuum. It works by a physical law which is analogous to a moral law. The rushing streams seek the mighty deeps. The waters are the daughters of the clouds and the mountains, and always set out for the valleys. True enjoyment comes from above, as we have already said: it is desire which attracts, and desire is a bottomless pit.

That which is not attracts that which is, hence those who are most unworthy of love are sometimes the most beloved. Fullness goes looking for a vacuum, and the vacuum sucks it in. Animals and wet-nurses know this well.

Pindar never loved Sappho, and Sappho had to resign herself to all the disdain of Phaon. A man and woman of genius are brother and sister: their mating would be a sort of incest; and a man who is merely a man will never fall in love with a 'bearded lady'.

Rousseau seems to have sensed this when he married a servant girl, a dull-witted and grasping virago. But he could never get Thérèse to realize his intellectual superiority, and he was obviously her inferior in the cruder aspects of existence. In their household Thérèse was the man and Rousseau was the woman. Rousseau was too proud to accept his position, and protested against Thérèse's regime by treating her children as foundlings. By doing so he set nature against him and exposed himself to the mother's revenge.

You men of genius, refrain from having children; your only legitimate offspring are your books. Never marry; reputation is your wife! Keep your virility for her; and, when you find a Heloise, do not expose yourselves to Abelard's fate for the sake of a woman!

CHAPTER VIII
The Astral Emanations and Magnetic Projections

A universe may be defined as a group of magnetized spheres which attract and repel one another. The beings produced by the different spheres share their special magnetization balanced by the universal magnetism.

Poorly balanced men are disordered or exaggerated magnets which nature weighs one against the other, until the partial error in balance has produced destruction.

Bunsen's spectrum analysis will enable science to distinguish the special features of the magnets and thus supply a scientific reason for the ancient rules of judicial astrology. The different planets of the system certainly exert a magnetic effect on our own globe and on the various constitutions of the living creatures which inhabit it.

We all absorb the celestial aromas mingled with the spirit of earth and born under the influence of diverse stars; we all have a preference for a force characterized by a particular form, for a certain bent and for a certain colour.

The Pythoness of Delphi, seated on a tripod over a crevice in the ground, drew in the astral fluid through her sexual parts, fell into a state of dementia or clairvoyance and uttered incoherent sentences which sometimes turned out to be oracles. All highly-strung natures abandoned to disorders of the passions resemble the Pythoness and breath in Python, that is to say, the evil and fatal spirit of the earth. Then they forcibly project the fluid which has penetrated them, inspiring and absorbing immediately afterwards the vital fluids of other beings; thus they exercise in rotation the malign powers, first of the evil eye and then of the vampire.

If these sick people who are suffering from this deleterious form of *inhaling* and *exhaling* take it for a power and wish to increase the accumulation and projection, they express their desires in ceremonies which are called evocations, and hoodoo, and become what were termed in former times necromancers and sorcerers.

Every appeal to some unknown and strange intelligence, whose existence has not been demonstrated, with the object of substituting its guidance for that of our own reason and of our own free will, may be looked on as intellectual suicide, for it is an appeal to folly.

Everything which resigns the will to mysterious forces, everything which makes other voices speak in us than the voices of conscience and reason, belongs to mental derangement.

The insane are static visionaries, a waking vision is a fit of madness. The art of evocation is the art of provoking an artificial fit of madness in oneself.

All visions have the nature of dreams and are illusions of unsound minds. They are clouds from a disordered imagination projected into the astral light; it is we ourselves who appear to ourselves disguised as phantoms, apparitions of the dead or as demons.

Crazed individuals seem to make nature herself delirious, within the circle of their attraction and magnetic projection: the furniture makes rapping noises and moves about, and light-weight articles are attracted or thrown at a distance. Mental specialists are well aware of this but are afraid to admit as much, because official science has not yet acknowledged that human beings can be magnets and that these magnets can be maladjusted out of order. The abbé Vianney, parish priest of Ars, believed he was being continually tormented by a demon's practical jokes; and Berbiguier, of Terre-Neuve du Thym, armed himself with long pins for sticking into goblins.

Now, the point of support exists in the resistance offered to them by undisciplined development. What renders the organization of an army impossible in democracy is that each soldier fancies himself a general. There is only one general with the Jesuits.

Obedience is the gymnastics of liberty, and before one can reach the point of doing always what one wants it is often necessary to learn to do what one does not want. What pleases us is to be in the service of fantasy; doing things we do not like is to exercise the reason and will and make them triumph.

Contraries assert and confirm themselves by contraries. Looking left when one wants to go right is an act of dissembling and prudence; but to throw some weights into the left-hand pan of the scales to make the right-hand pan rise, is to know the laws of dynamics and equilibrium.

It is the resistance which determines the quantity of the force in dynamics; but there is no resistance which cannot be worn down by persistent effort and movement: this is how the mouse gnaws through the rope and the drops of water pierce the rock.

Effort which is renewed daily builds force up and conserves it, even if the action is applied to something which is indifferent in itself or unreasonable and ridiculous into the bargain. It is hardly a serious-looking occupation to pass the beads of a rosary between one's fingers while repeating 'Hail Mary!' two or three hundred times. All the same, if a monk gets to bed without going through the rosary, he will wake up next day feeling very low, with no courage to offer the morning prayer and will be inattentive during Divine Service. Therefore the monks' confessors will keep reminding them, and with good reason, not to neglect the little things.

The grimoires and magic rituals are full of directions which are detailed and, on the face of it, ridiculous:

Eat your food without salt for ten or twenty days, sleep propped on your elbow,. sacrifice a black cock at midnight at a crossroads in the middle of a forest, go to a graveyard and take a fistful of earth from a freshly occupied grave, etc., then shroud yourself in certain bizarre vestments and pronounce long and tedious conjurations. Were the authors of these books trying to make fun of their readers? Were they imparting genuine secrets to them? No, they were not joking, and their information was serious. Their object was to exalt the imagination of their adepts and to make them conscious of a supplementary force which exists as soon as one believes in it and always grows stronger with persistent effort. Only, it can happen by the law of the reaction of contraries that the devil is evoked by unremitting prayer to God, and that after satanic conjurations one hears the angels weep. All hell danced with bells when St Anthony recited the Psalms, and Paradise seemed to revive again before the enchantments of Albertus Magnus or Merlin.

It is because ceremonies in themselves mean very little, and everything depends on the *inhaling* and the *exhaling*. The formulas consecrated by long usage, place us in communication with the living and the dead, and when our will enters like this into the great currents it is able to arm itself with all their emanations. A servant-girl who practises may, at a given moment, deploy all the temporal might of the Church with the support of the arms of France, as was clearly shown at the time of the baptism and abduction of the Jew Mortara. All civilized Europe, in the nineteenth century protested against this act, and suffered it because a devout housemaid had willed it. But earth sent as auxiliaries to this girl the spectral emanations of the eras of Saint Dominic and Torquemada; Saint Ghislieri prayed for her. The shade of the great king who revoked the edict of Nantes gave her a sign of approbation, and the entire clerical world was ready to uphold her.

Joan of Arc, who was burnt as a witch, had in fact attracted to her the spirit of heroic France, and poured it out in a marvellous manner to electrify its army and put the English to flight. A pope rehabilitated her; it was not enough, it was necessary to canonize her. If this thaumaturge was no sorcerer she was plainly a saint. What is a sorcerer anyway? Only a thaumaturge who does not meet with the pope's approval.

Miracles are, if I may be allowed to say so, extravagances of nature produced by the excited emotions of man. They always follow the same laws. Any popular celebrity could work miracles, sometimes in fact without willing it. At the time when France idolized its kings, the French kings cured scrofula, and, in our own days the immense popularity of those picturesque and barbarian soldiers called zouaves has developed in a zouave named Jacob the faculty of healing with voice and eye. We hear that this zouave has left his corps to join the grenadiers, and we look on it as certain that the grenadier Jacob will no longer have the power which was the exclusive property of the zouave.

In Druid times, in Gaul, there were female thaumaturges called elves and fairies. To the Druids they were saints; to the Christians they were sorcerers. Joseph Balsamo, known as the divine Cagliostro to his disciples, was condemned at Rome as a heretic and warlock, for having performed miracles and issued predictions without leave from the Ordinary. Now in this the inquisitors were correct, since the Roman Church held the monopoly of High Magic and effective ceremonies. She charms demons with water and salt; she evokes God with bread and wine to gain His visible and palpable presence on earth; she uses oil to bestow health and pardon.

She does more: she creates priests and kings.

She alone understands and reveals why the kings from the triple realm of magic, the three magi, led by the blazing star, came to offer to Jesus Christ in His cradle, the gold which fascinates the eyes and conquers men's hearts, the frankincense which lifts asceticism to the brain, and the myrrh which preserves dead bodies and renders palpable, to some extent, the doctrine of immortality by showing inviolability and incorruption in death.

CHAPTER IX
The Magical Sacrifice

First of all, we shall discuss sacrifice in general.

What is sacrifice? It may be defined as the practical expression of devotion.

It is the substitution of the innocent for the guilty, in the voluntary work of expiation.

It is the generously unfair payment made by the just (who undergoes the punishment) for the dastardly injustice of the rebel (who stole a pleasure in which he had no right).

It is the temperance of the wise man, which acts as a counterweight in the universal life to the orgies of the senseless.

Such is sacrifice in reality, and such are the leading characteristics it must always preserve.

In the ancient world, sacrifice was rarely voluntary. The offender devoted to suffering what he regarded as his by right of conquest or right of property.

Now, black magic is the occult continuation of the proscribed rites of the ancient world. Immolation lies at the bottom of the mysteries of necromancy, and witchcraft with wax figures is equivalent to magical sacrifices where the evil magnetism is substituted for the faggot and the knife. In religion it is faith which saves; in black magic it is faith which kills!

We have already explained that black magic is the religion of death.

To die in another's place is the sublime sacrifice. To kill someone else to avoid death is the sacrifice of impiety. To consent to the murder of the innocent to secure impunity for our own misdeeds would be the final and most unforgivable act of cowardice, if the victim's offering were not voluntary and if this victim had not the right to offer himself as our superior and his own absolute master. This has been considered the indispensable condition for human redemption.

We are speaking here of a belief consecrated by many centuries of adoration and by the faith of millions of men and women; and as we have said that the collective and persistent word creates whatever it affirms, we are entitled to say that so it is.

Now, the sacrifice of the cross is renewed and perpetuated in that of the altar; and there, perhaps, it fills the believer with even greater awe. The divine victim is found there without even human form; he is mute and passive, given up to those who wish to take him, unresisting in the face of those who dare to desecrate him. He is a white and fragile host. He comes at the call of a bad priest and will not protest if the intention is to involve him in the most impure rites. Before Christianity appeared, the Stryges ate the flesh of slaughtered children; now they content themselves with consecrated wafers.

People are blind to the superhuman power of wickedness open to the evil votaries who abuse the sacraments. Nothing is so malignant as a communicant from the gutter press. 'He is full of bad wine', is said of the drunkard who beats his wife when he is tipsy. I once heard a so-called Catholic say that he had the God of evil. It seems that a second transubstantiation takes place in the mouths of certain communicants. God has been placed on their tongues, but it is the Devil whom they swallow.

A Catholic host is a really fearsome thing. It contains the whole of Heaven and Hell, because it is charged with the magnetism of centuries and of multitudes: a good magnetism when it is approached with true faith, a magnetism of concentrated evil when it is put to an unworthy use. Besides, nothing is so sought after and considered so powerful for casting evil spells as hosts consecrated by lawful priests, but diverted from their pious destination by sacrilegious theft.

We are descending here into the depths of the horrors of black magic, and let no-one suppose that in exposing them we wish to encourage these abominable practices.

Gilles de Laval, lord of Retz, had the Black Mass celebrated by an apostate Dominican friar, in a secret chapel at his castle of Machecoul. At the elevation a little child was slaughtered, and the field-marshal communicated with a fragment of the host soaked in the victim's blood.

The author of the grimoire of Honorius says that the person who performs works of black magic must be a priest. According

to him, the best ceremonies for evoking the devil are those of
Catholic worship and, in fact, on Father Ventura's own
confession, the devil is born from the working of this way of
worship. In a letter addressed to Mr Gougenot Des Mousseaux
and published by the latter at the beginning of one of his
principal works, the learned Theatine monk has not scrupled to
state that the devil is the fool of the Catholic religion (at least as
far as father Ventura understands it). Here are his own words:

> Satan, said Voltaire, is Christianity; no Satan, no Christianity. So it follows
> that Satan's masterpiece is to be a success by getting his existence denied. By
> demonstrating the existence of Satan we restore one of the fundamental
> doctrines on which Christianity is based and without which it is only a word.
> (Letter from Father Ventura to the Chevalier Gougenot Des Mousseaux
> prefacing his book *La Magie au XIXe siècle (Magic up to the nineteenth century)*.

Thus, after Proudhon had the effrontery to say 'God is evil', a
priest who is supposed to be well-informed caps the thought of
the atheist by saying: Christianity is Satan. And he says this in all
simplicity, under the impression that he is defending the religion
which he libels in such an appalling way, misrepresenting it like
the simony and material considerations which have plunged some
members of the clergy into a black caricature of Christianity, that
of Gilles de Laval and of the grimoire of Honorius. Perhaps it
was the same father who said to the Pope: 'We must not
jeopardize the Kingdom of Heaven for a clod of earth'. In
himself, Father Ventura is a decent man, and at times the true
Christian in him gets the better of the monk and priest.

If one can concentrate on an agreed point and fasten all one's
aspirations for good on a sign, one has enough faith to realize
God in this sign. Such is the permanent miracle which takes place
every day on the altars of true Christianity.

The same sign, when profaned and consecrated to evil, is
capable of realizing evil in the same manner, and if the justified
man is able to say, after his communion, Jesus Christ lives in me,
or to put it another way: I am myself no longer, I am Jesus
Christ, I am one with God; even the unworthy communicant can
say with no less certitude and truth: I am no longer I, I am Satan.

To create Satan and to turn into Satan, this is the great arcana
of black magic, and this is what the accomplice sorcerers of the
lord of Retz thought they were accomplishing for him; and they

did accomplish it for him, up to a certain point, by saying the devil's Mass.

Would man ever have been in danger of creating the devil, if he had never had the temerity to want to create God by giving Him a body? Have we not said that a corporeal God must necessarily cast a shadow, and that that shadow is Satan? Yes, these were our words, and we shall never say the contrary. But if the body of God is imaginary, then His shadow could not possibly be real.

The divine body is only an appearance, a veil, a cloud: Jesus knew this by faith. Let us pay homage to the Light and not give reality to the shadow, for the latter is not the object of our faith! It is the will of nature, and will always be her will, that religion shall exist on the earth. Religion germinates, flowers and fructifies in man; it is the fruit of his aspirations and his desires; it has to be governed by sovereign reason. But the aspirations of man towards the infinite, his longings for eternal good and his reason in particular, come from God!

CHAPTER X
Evocations

Reason alone gives the right to liberty. Liberty and reason, these two great and essential privileges of mankind, are so closely united that one cannot be renounced unless the use of the other is also given up. Liberty wills the triumph of reason and reason imperiously demands the reign of liberty. Liberty and reason are more important that life itself to man. It is beautiful to die for liberty, and it is sublime to be a martyr for reason, because reason and liberty are the very essence of the soul's immortality.

God Himself is the free reason of all that exists.

The devil, on the other hand, is fatal irrationalism.

To forswear one's reason or one's liberty is to disown God. To make any appeal to what is irrational or fatalistic is to evoke the devil. We have already said that the devil does exist, and that he is a thousand times more horrible and pitiless than the legends describe him, even at their most gruesome. For us and for reason, he could not possibly be the fine fallen angel of Milton, nor flashing Lucifer, trailing his starry glory through the night with here and there the glitter of lightning. Such titanic fables are impious. The true devil is the one sculptured in our cathedrals and depicted by the naive illuminators of our Gothic books. His essentially hybrid form is the synthesis of all nightmares; it is hideous, deformed and grotesque. He is fettered and binds others in fetters. He has eyes everywhere, except in his head; he has faces in his stomach, in his knees, and on his unspeakably filthy rump. He is everywhere where folly can find a footing, and everywhere he drags behind him the torments of hell.

He himself does not utter a syllable, but he makes all our vices speak; he is the ventriloquist who operates the gluttons, the Python of abandoned women. At times his voice is as impetuous as the whirlwind, at times it is as insinuating as a low hiss. To converse with our troubled brains he inserts his forked tongue into our ears and to undo our hearts he shakes his tail like an arrow. In our head he slays reason, in our hearts he poisons liberty, and he does this always and of necessity unremittingly, because he is not a person but a blind force; he is accursed, but accursed with us; he is a sinner, but he sins in us. We alone are responsible for the evil which he makes us do, because as for him, he has neither liberty nor reason.

The devil is the beast; Saint John hammers this home in his marvellous Apocalypse; but how can one comprehend the Apocalypse without the keys of the holy Qabalah?

An evocation, therefore, is an appeal to the beast, and only the beast can respond. We might add that to make the beast appear one must first form it within oneself and then project it outside. This secret is that of all the grimoires, but it was only expressed by the ancient masters in a very veiled manner.

To see the devil it is necessary to make oneself up like the devil and then look in a mirror. This is the secret in its simplicity, so that even a child could understand it. Let us add for the benefit of men that, in the mysteries of sorcerers, the devilish countenance is imprinted on the soul by the astral intermediary, and the mirror is darkness animated as the head reels.

Every evocation would be in vain if the magician did not commence by damning his soul in sacrificing for ever his liberty and his reason. It is easy to understand this. To create the beast in us it is essential to kill the man; which is what was represented previously by the sacrifice of a child, and even more distinctly by the profanation of a host. The man who elects to perform an evocation is a wretch who is embarrassed by reason and wishes to magnify in himself the bestial appetites, so that he can turn them into a magnetic centre endowed with a fatal influence. He wishes to personify unreason and fatalism; he wishes to become a disordered magnet, and an evil one too, to attract to himself the vices and the gold which feed them. It is the most terrible crime which the imagination could dream of. It is the rape of nature. It is the direct and absolute outrage thrown in the face of divinity; but also, and happily so, it is a frightfully difficult task, and most of those who have attempted it have come unstuck in the accomplishment. If a man who was strong enough and perverse enough were to evoke the devil in the required conditions, the devil would materialize. God would be held back and terror-stricken nature would be subjected to the despotism of evil.

It is said that years ago a certain man undertook this monstrous work and that he became pope. It is also related that on his death-bed he confessed to enveloping the whole Church in a web of black magic. One thing is certain: this pope was as deeply instructed as Faust, and it is claimed he was the author of several wonderful inventions. We have mentioned him already in one of our books. However, the proof, according to the legend itself, that he did not evoke the devil, that is to say, did not become the devil, is his repentance. The devil never repents.

The reason why the majority of men are mediocrities, is that they are always incomplete. Decent people sometimes do wrong, and scoundrels forget themselves at times to the extent of forming some good wish which they carry out. Now, sins against God weaken the power of God in man, and sins against the devil (by which I mean good desires and deeds) weaken the power of the devil. To exercise any exceptional power either above or below, on the right hand or the left hand, it is essential to be a whole man.

Fear and remorse in criminals are two things which originate from good, and these lead them to betray themselves. To succeed in wickedness one has to be absolutely wicked. We are assured that Mandrin heard confession from his brigands, and gave them as a penance the murder of some child or woman when they admitted to him that they had felt some pity. Nero had some good in him, he was an artistic performer, and this was his undoing. He gave up, and committed suicide in vexation at being underrated as a musician. If he had been nothing more than an emperor he would have burnt Rome a second time sooner than give way to the Senate and to Vindex; the people were on his side; he had only to shower them with gold and the praetors would have acclaimed him once more. Nero's suicide was the action of an artist trying to show off.

To succeed in turning himself into Satan would not be a complete triumph for human perversity, if immortality were not won at the same time. Prometheus can take the suffering on his rock; he knows that one day his chain will be broken and that he will dethrone Jupiter; but to be Prometheus one has to have stolen the fire of heaven, and we are not yet in reach of the fire of hell!

No, the dream of Satan is not that of Prometheus. If a rebel angel had ever been able to snatch the fire of heaven, that is to say the divine secret of life, he would be like God. Only man is sufficiently stupid and limited in intelligence to believe in the existence of a possible solution to this sort of theorem: to make what is what is not, at one and the same time; to make shadow light, death life, a lie the truth, and nothingness everything. Besides, the wild idiot who wants to realize the absolute in evil will end at last, like the careless alchemist, in a tremendous explosion which will bury him in the wreckage of his ridiculous laboratory.

An instantaneous and overwhelming death has resulted at times from infernal evocations, and one cannot help admitting that it was only too well deserved. One does not go with impunity to the limits of extreme lunacy. There are certain excesses that nature will not countenance. If sleep-walkers have sometimes died when woken with a start, if a certain degree of drunkenness causes death ... But perhaps someone will ask, what use are these retrospective warnings – who in this day and age would dream of making evocations with a grimoire ritual? We have no reply to make to this question, for if we told everything we knew it is likely that no-one would believe us!

There are also other ways of evoking the magnetism of evil than by the rituals of the ancient world. We said in our last chapter that a Mass profaned by criminal intentions becomes an outrage offered to God and an offence by the man against his own conscience. Consulting oracles, either when the head swims in a state of hallucination, or by noting the uncontrolled movements of inert objects magnetized at random, are also forms of infernal evocation, because they are acts which tend to subordinate liberty and reason to fate. It is true that those who carry out the instructions in books of black magic are nearly always innocent by their very ignorance. They make their appeal to the beast, it is true, but it is not the ferocious beast which would serve their lusts they want. They are only asking advice of the stupid beast, as a little assistance for their own stupidity.

In the magic of light, the science of evocations is the art of magnetizing the currents in the astral light and of directing them at will. This science was that practised by Zoroaster and King Solomon, if one can believe the old traditions; but to do what was done by Zoroaster and Solomon, it is necessary to have the wisdom of Solomon and the learning of Zoroaster.

To direct and dominate the magnetism of good, it is requisite to be the best of men. To activate and precipitate the vortex of evil it is necessary to be the worst. Sincere Catholics do not doubt that the prayers of a poor recluse can change the mind of kings and settle the destinies of empires. We are far from scorning this belief, we who admit that life is collective, who acknowledge the magnetic currents and the relative omnipotence of the will.

Before the recent scientific discoveries, the phenomena of electricity and magnetism were attributed to spirits diffused in the atmosphere, and the adept who managed to influence the magnetic currents thought he was commanding spirits. But since the magnetic currents are fatalistic forces, one has to be a perfectly balanced centre oneself before one can control and balance them, which can hardly be said of the majority of these reckless sorcerers.

They were also often struck down in a violent flash by the imponderable fluid, which they were unable to neutralize. They admitted, too, that they lacked the indispensable thing for gaining absolute mastery over spirits: the Ring of Solomon.

But according to legend the ring of Solomon is still on that monarch's finger, and his body is shut up in a rock which will not break open until the last judgement.

Like all legends, this one is true. All it needs is understanding.

What is meant by the ring? — a ring is the end of a chain, a circle to which other circles may be fastened.

Chief priests have always worn rings as a sign of their authority over the circle and over the chain of the faithful.

In our own days prelates are still invested with the ring; and, in the marriage service, the bridegroom gives the bride a ring which has been blessed and consecrated by the Church, in order to make her the mistress and controller of his household affairs and of his circle of servants.

Hence the pontifical ring and the wedding ring which has been consecrated and conferred hierarchically, represent and bring into being a certain power.

But public and social power is one thing, sympathetic, philosophical and occult power is another.

Solomon is supposed to have been sovereign pontiff of the religion of the initiates, which gave him the right to the royal prerogative of the occult priesthood, for he possessed — so it is said — universal knowledge, and in him alone was realized the promise of the great serpent: 'Ye shall be as gods, knowing good and evil.'

Some say that Solomon wrote Ecclesiastes, the most rationalist of all his works, after worshipping Astarte and Chamos, the gods of heathen women he had married. In this way he would have completed his knowledge and rediscovered the magic virtue of his ring before he died. Did he really take it with him into the tomb? Another legend introduces an element of doubt at this point. It tells how the Queen of Sheba, after examining this ring with great care, had an exactly similar one made secretly; and how, while the king slept, she chanced to be near him and was able to carry out a furtive exchange of rings. She went home to the Sabeans with the true ring of Solomon, and this ring was later found by Zoroaster.

It was a gem-encrusted ring, composed of the seven great metals, and bearing the signature of the seven spirits, with a rose-red lodestone having the usual seal of Solomon engraved on one side:

and his magic seal engraved on the other:

Those who have read our books will understand this allegory.

CHAPTER XI
The Arcana of Solomon's Ring

You must look in Solomon's tomb, that is to say, in the crypts of occult philosophy, not for his ring but for his wisdom.

Assisted by wisdom and a persistent will, you will attain wisdom's supreme secret, which is free sovereignty over balanced movement. You will then be able to get the ring for yourself by having it made by a goldsmith, to whom you will have no occasion to reveal the secret. For if he does not know what he is making he will not be able to tell others.

Here is the formula for the ring:

Take a small quantity of gold and twice the amount of silver at the hours of the sun and the moon, and mix them together; add three parts similar to the first of well refined copper, four parts of tin, five of iron, six of mercury and seven of lead. Mix them all together at the hours corresponding to the metals, and make the whole into a ring with the circular part flattened and slightly broad, permitting characters to be engraved on it.

Make a square setting in this ring to hold a red lodestone mounted in a double ring of gold.

Engrave the double seal of Solomon on the stone, above and below.

Engrave the ring with the occult signs of the seven planets as illustrated in the magical Archidoxis of Paracelsus or in Agrippa's Occult Philosophy; magnetize the ring strongly by consecrating it every day for a week with the ceremonies appointed in our ritual.

The ring must then be wrapped in a silk fabric and, after fumigation, may be carried on your person.

A round piece of metal or a talisman prepared in the same manner would have as much virtue as the ring.

Anything prepared like this is a sort of reservoir of the will. It is a magnetic reflector which can prove very useful, although it is never essential.

We have stated elsewhere that the ancient rites have lost their efficacy since the advent of Christianity.

Catholic Christianity is in fact the legitimate daughter of Jesus, whom the magi adored. Catholic worship is nothing other than high magic referred to the laws of the hierarchy, which are indispensable to ensure that it is both reasonable and efficacious.

An ordinary scapular, worn by a true Christian, is a more invincible talisman than the ring and the pentacle of Solomon.

Jesus Christ, Son of God and Son of Man, so humble, said of Himself: 'The Queen of Sheba came from the distant East to see and listen to Solomon, and a greater than Solomon is here.'

The Mass is the most prodigious of evocations.

Necromancers evoke the dead, sorcerers evoke the devil and tremble, but the Catholic priest does not tremble to evoke the Living God!

What are all the talismans of ancient science in comparison with the consecrated wafer?

Let Solomon's skeleton sleep on in its tomb of rock, together with the ring he may have on his bony finger. Jesus Christ has risen from the dead, He lives. Take one of those silver rings as sold at the church porch, stamped with the image of the crucified and with ten rosary beads. If you are worthy to wear it, it will be more effective in your hands than the genuine ring of Solomon would be.

Magical rituals and detailed performances in worship are all for the ignorant and superstitious, and we cannot help recalling the well-known story which we shall now relate briefly, because it fits in here.

Two monks entered a thatched cottage which had been left in the care of two children, and asked to be allowed to rest and to have something to eat if that were possible. The children replied that they had nothing to give.

– 'Ah well!' said one of the monks, 'here's a fire; just lend us a pot and a little water and we'll make ourselves some soup.'

'With what?'

'With this pebble', said the cunning friar, fetching a piece of stone. 'Don't you know, my children, that the disciples of St Francis possess the secret of pebble soup?'

Pebble soup? What a marvel for the children! They were promised that they would taste it and find it excellent.

Within the space of a few minutes the pot was got ready, the water was poured into it, the fire was stirred into a blaze, and the pebble was carefully placed in the water.

'So far so good,' said the monks, 'and now a little salt and some vegetables; bring them, there are some in your garden. Now, why not add a little smoked bacon? It will only improve the soup.'

The children squatted by the hearth looking on in wonder. The pot boiled.

'Right, cut a few slices of bread and come to this tureen. My! What a smell! Lay the table, and let's dip our bread in the soup. Here's the pebble, wrap it up carefully, you may keep it for your trouble; it will never be used up and will always work. Now then, taste the soup! There! What did we tell you?'

'Oh! It's first rate!' said the little peasant children, clapping their hands.

In fact it was a good bacon and cabbage soup, which the children would never have managed to set before their guests without the bit of wonder-working with the pebble.

Magical rituals and religious ceremonies are rather like the monks' pebble. They supply the pretext and the occasion for practising virtues which, in themselves, are indispensable to the moral life of man. The good monks would not have dined without the pebble; so did some real power reside in the stone? Yes, in the imagination of the youngsters, which was set working by the ingenuity of the good fathers.

We can say this without blaming or offending anyone. The monks were sensible men, not liars. They helped the children to do good, and filled them with admiration, helping them to share a good soup; and in this connection we advise those who are feeling hungry but would find it rather too difficult (or rather too simple) to make cabbage soup, to make pebble soup instead.

We want to be clearly understood on this point. We are not trying to say that signs and rites are a big piece of humbug. They would be such if people did not need them; but we have to recognize that everyone has not the same degree of intelligence. Children have always had fairy stories told to them, and these stories will continue to be told as long as there are nurses and mothers. Children have faith and this is what saves them. Imagine a child of seven saying: 'I do not want to accept anything I cannot understand.' What could one teach such a monster? Accept what your teachers tell you to begin with, my fine fellow, then study it and, if you are not an idiot, you will understand it by-and-by.

Children need fables, the masses need fables and ceremonies; the frailty of mankind needs crutches. Blessed are those who possess the ring of Solomon, but even more blessed are those who equal or surpass Solomon in knowledge and wisdom without requiring his ring!

CHAPTER XII
The Terrible Secret

Some truths will ever remain mysterious for the slow-witted and the foolish; and we need not be afraid to tell them these truths, because it is quite certain that they will never understand them.

What is a fool? One who is somewhat more irrational than a dumb animal. He is a man who wants to run before he can crawl; a man who thinks he has mastered a subject as soon as he had made a little progress in it; a mathematician who looks down his nose at poetry; a poet who condemns mathematics; a painter who says that theology and the Qabalah are stuff and nonsense; an uneducated man who repudiates knowledge without taking the trouble to study it; a man who talks without knowing what he is talking about and makes assertions without certainty. Fools are the people who kill men of genius. Galileo was not condemned by the Church, but by the fools who, unfortunately, belonged to the Church. Folly is a wild beast which has the composure of innocence; it assassinates without remorse. The fool is the bear in La Fontaine's fable; he breaks his friend's head under a paving-stone to whisk away a fly; but do not try to make him admit he is at fault when things go badly wrong. Folly, like Hell and Fate, is inexorable and infallible, because it is always controlled by the magnetism of evil.

The animal is never a fool, because it openly and naturally plays the role of an animal; but man teaches folly to dogs and intelligent donkeys. The fool is the animal who despises instinct and poses as intelligent.

Progress is a possibility for the animal: it can be broken in, tamed and trained; but it is not a possibility for the fool, because the fool thinks he has nothing to learn. It is his place to dictate to others and put them right, and so it is impossible to reason with him. He will laugh you to scorn in saying that what he does not understand is not a meaningful proposition. 'Why don't I understand it, then?', he asks you, with marvellous impudence. To tell him it is because he is a fool would only be taken as an insult, so there is nothing you can say in reply. Everybody else sees it quite clearly, but he will never realize it.

Here then, at the outset, is a potent secret which is inaccessible to the majority of people; a secret which they will never guess and which it would be useless to tell them: the secret of their own stupidity.

Socrates had to drink hemlock, Aristotle was banished, Jesus was crucified, Aristophanes mocked Socrates and made the fools of Athens laugh at him, a country bumpkin got tired of hearing Aristides called the Just, and Renan wrote his 'Life of Jesus' for the delectation of fools. It is owing to the almost infinite number of fools that politics is and always will be the science of double-dealing and lies. Machiavelli dared to make this known and has been quite rightly censured, for under the pretence of giving lessons to princes he betrayed them all and exposed them to the mistrust of the masses. It is important not to alert those whom one is forced to deceive.

Jesus was thinking of the base and silly masses when he said to His disciples: 'Do not throw pearls to pigs, because they will tread on them with their trotters and turn on you to tear you to pieces.'

You, then, who want to do great things, never tell anybody your inmost thoughts, not even that wife you love; and I might almost say hide them chiefly from her — remember the story of Samson and Delilah!

As soon as a wife knows her husband through and through she stops loving him. She wants to control him and manage him. If he resists her she hates him; if he surrenders she despises him. She looks round for some other man she can probe into. Women always need the unknown and the mysterious, and their love is often nothing more than an insatiable curiosity.

Why do confessors hold such total sway over the souls, and nearly always over the hearts, of women? It is because they know all their secrets, while the women do not know those of their confessors.

Freemasonry is only so powerful in the world because of its dread secret, so wonderfully well kept that the initiates, even those who are in the highest degrees, do not know it.

The Catholic religion keeps its hold on the masses by a secret unknown to the Pope himself. It is the secret of the mysteries. The old Gnostics knew it, as indicated by their name, but they did not know how to keep silent. They wanted to popularize gnosis, and came out with ridiculous doctrines which the Church was right to condemn. Unhappily, when they were condemned, so was the entrance to the occult sanctuary and the portal keys were hurled into the abyss.

Into that pit the Hospitallers and Templars dared to go to fetch them, at the risk of eternal damnation. Did they deserve to be damned for this in the other world? We only know that in this world the Templars were burned at the stake.

The secret doctrine of Jesus was this:

People have looked on God as overlord, and evil as the prince of this world; I, who am the Son of God, tell you: Do not go looking for God out in space, He is in our consciences and in our hearts. My Father and I are completely One, and I wish you and Me to be only one also. Let us love one another like brothers. Have only one heart and one soul. The religious law was made for man, not man for the law. The legal prescriptions are brought to the free arbitration of our reason united with faith. Believe in what is good and evil will not have you in its power.

When you come together in my Name, my Spirit will be in the midst of you. No one of you must imagine that he is the master of the others, but all must respect the decision of the assembly. Every man has to be judged by his works, and measured according to the measure he himself adopts when measuring. Each man's conscience comprises his faith, it is the power of God in him.

If you have mastered yourself, nature will obey you and you will govern the others. The faith of the just is more unshakeable than the gates of Hell, and their hope shall never be confounded.

I am you and you me, in the spirit of love which is ours, and is God. Believe this and your word will be creative. Believe this and you will perform miracles. The world will persecute you, and you will overcome the world.

The good are those who show charity and those who help the afflicted; the wicked are the hearts which are pitiless, and these will be eternally reprobated by humanity and reason.

The old forms of society, founded on falsehood shall perish; one day the Son of Man shall be enthroned above the clouds of Heaven, which are the shades of idolatry, and will pronounce a final judgement on the living and the dead.

Desire the light, for it will shine forth. Aspire after justice, for it will come. Do not seek to triumph by the sword, for murder begets murder. It is by patience and gentleness that you will become masters of yourselves and of the world.

Now read this admirable teaching in the commentaries of the sophists during the era of decadence and in those of the quibblers of the Middle Ages, and you will see some strange things extracted from it. — If Jesus was the Son of God, how did God beget Him? Has He the same substance as God, or has He a different substance? The substance of God! What an eternal subject of dispute for presumptuous ignorance! Was He a divine person or a human person? Did He have two natures and two wills? Terrible questions these, which certainly merit excommunication or a slit throat! — 'Jesus had one nature and two wills', said one party, but do not listen to them, they are heretics! 'Two natures, then, and one will?' — 'No, two wills'. — 'Then He was in opposition to Himself?' 'No, for these two wills only made one, which is called Theandric.' — Ah, yes! In the face of this word we must say no more, especially as we have to obey the Church, which has changed into something quite different from the primitive assembly of the faithful. Jesus said that the law is made for man, but the Church says that man is made for the Church, and it is she who imposes the law. God will ratify all the decrees of the Church and will damn you all if she decides that you are all, or nearly all, of you damned. Jesus said you have to agree with the assembly, therefore it is infallible, therefore it is God, therefore if it makes up its mind that two and two make five, two and two shall make five.

If it says that the earth is still and the sun goes round it, the earth is forbidden to turn. It will tell you that God saves His elect by giving them enabling grace, and that the remainder will be damned for only receiving sufficient grace, which is sufficient in principle but is actually insufficient because of original sin; it will also inform you that the Pope saves and damns whom he pleases, since he has the keys of Heaven and Hell. Then along come the casuists with their bunches of keys which do not open, but double and triple lock all the doors of all the suites of rooms planned in the Tower of Babel. O Rabelais, my master, you alone can bring a suitable panacea for all this mental aberration! An enormous peal of laughter! Come, sum all this up in one last word for us, and inform us whether a bag of wind which goes pop in a vacuum can be blown up a second time and ballasted with the marvellous quiddity of our second intentions?'

Utrum chimaera in vacuum bombinans possit concidere secundum intentiones?

Other fools, other commentaries. Here come the adversaries of the Church who tell us: God is in man, which means that there is no other God than the human intellect. If man is above the religious law and finds it inconvenient, why not suppress the law? If God is us and we are brothers, all of us, if nobody has the right to set himself up as our master, why should we obey? Faith is the reason of imbeciles. Believe nothing and submit to no-one.

That's right! Be high and mighty. But you will have to fight it out, all against all and each against each. This is the war of the gods and the extermination of the human race! Alas! alas! misery and folly! ... Then more and more folly; folly and misery!

'Father, forgive them,' said Jesus, 'for they know not what they do' – People of good sense whoever you may be, I will add, do not listen to them, for they know not what they say.

In that case they are innocent, some *enfant terrible* will exclaim. – Silence, thoughtless one! Silence, in the name of Heaven, or all morality is lost! Besides, you are mistaken. If they were innocent it would be permissible to do as they do, and would you wish to imitate them? Total credulity is a folly; so it is not possible for folly to be innocent. If there are any extenuating circumstances, only God can make allowances for them.

Our species is obviously defective, and from what one hears and sees the majority of men behave as if they were not possessed of sufficient brains to be genuinely responsible. Listen to the parliamentary debates of the men whom France (the first country in the world) has honoured with her confidence.

There stands the spokesman for the opposition. Here is the minister. Each of them proves conclusively to the other that he understands absolutely nothing about affairs of State. A proves that B is a cretin, and B proves that A is a mountebank. Whom should one believe? If you are white, you will believe A; if you are red, you will believe B. But the truth, the truth! – The truth is that A and B are two charlatans and two liars; seeing that the claims of both are doubtful, each has been able to show that the other's position is worthless. I admire their proofs, and I admire the pair of them for the way they have demolished each other. Folk can find anything they like in books, except often what the author was trying to say. Folk laugh at religion, but send their children to church. Folk make a great pretence of cynicism, and yet they are superstitious. What people fear above all is common sense, truth and reason.

Childish vanity and sordid interest lead human beings by the nose until death, the final oblivion, the last laugh. Vanity lies at the bottom of most souls. Well, what is vanity? It is emptiness. Multiply zero by itself as many times as you like and it will always be zero, add up noughts and you will get nothing, nothing, nothing. Nothing, that is what the majority of men have planned for.

And these are the immortals! These souls so ridiculously deceiving and deceived are imperishable! For all these unthinking individuals Life is a supreme fall-trap over Hell! Oh! There is certainly a terrible secret as far as that is concerned: it is that of responsibility. The father answers for the children, the master for his servants, and the intelligent man for the unintelligent herd. Redemption comes through all superior men; folly suffers, but only the spirit atones.

The pain of a crushed worm or of a lacerated oyster cannot expiate.

Know then, O thou who wishest to be initiated into the great mysteries, that thou makest a pact with suffering and encounterest Hell. The vulture which gorged itself on Prometheus' entrails has fixed its eye upon thee, and the Furies, led by Mercury, are preparing the blocks of wood and the nails. Thou shalt be sacred, that is to say, consecrated to torment. Humanity has need of thine agonies.

Christ died as a young man on a cross, and all those whom He has initiated have been martyrs. Apollonius of Tyana died of the tortures inflicted on him in the prisons of Rome. Paracelsus and Agrippa led wanderer's lives and died wretchedly. William Postel died a prisoner. Saint-Germain and Cagliostro met a mysterious and probably tragic end. Sooner or later the pact has to be satisfied, either formally or tacitly. Compensation must be paid by every plunderer of the fruit of the tree of knowledge. It is necessary to free oneself from the tax nature has put on miracles. A final battle with the Devil has to be faced when one ventures to be as God.

*Eritis sicut dii scientes bonum et malum.**

* Ye shall be as gods, knowing good and evil.

BOOK THREE

The Sacerdotal Mystery
or the Art of being served by Spirits

CHAPTER I
Aberrant Forces

A vague feeling which could be termed a sense of the infinite activates and torments mankind. Man feels dormant forces lying inside him, and thinks he can detect the presence of amorphous foes and unknown helpers. Many times he needs to believe in the absurd and attempt the impossible. Perhaps he feels low and discouraged, baffled at every turn, and longing to twist his despair into the shape of some new hope. He has been deceived in love, his friends have deserted him, and reason is not enough to meet his case. A philosopher would depress him; a magician would scare him; so at this juncture he betakes himself to a priest!

The priest is the tamer of imaginary hippogryphs and monsters hatched by fantasy. He draws a force from our weaknesses and constructs a reality out of our chimeras: he is the homoeopathic doctor for human folly. Besides, is he not something more than a mere man? Is not his mission a legitimate one, nobly descended from Calvary or Sinai? I am referring to the Catholic priest now, and as a matter of fact he is the only one that exists. The Jews have their rabbis, the Moslems their imams, the Hindus their brahmins, the Chinese their bonzes, and the Protestants their ministers. Only the Catholics have priests, because only they have the altar and the sacrifice, that is to say, the sum total of religion.

To perform high magic is to set oneself up as a rival to the Catholic priesthood; to be a non-conformist priest in fact. Rome is the grand Thebes of the new initiation. In former times she raked up the bones of her martyrs to fight against the gods evoked by Julian. Her catacombs are her crypts, her rosaries and medals are her talismans, her congregations are her magic chains, her magnetic sources are her convents, her centres of attraction are her confessionals. As means of expansion she has her sees, her printing presses and the pastoral letters of her bishops. Finally, she has her pope, the 'god-man' made visible and permanent on earth; her pope, who may be a fool as nearly all fanatics are, more or less, or a scoundrel like Alexander VI, who for all that will be the governor of spirits, the arbiter of conscience, and the legitimate bestower of indulgences and pardons throughout the Christian world.

That is ridiculous, you will say! — Yes, it borders on the ridiculous because of its magnitude! It borders on the ridiculous because it goes beyond the sublime! What comparable power has ever appeared on this earth; and if it did not exist, who would ever dare to invent it? What is the origin of this prodigy which seems to achieve the impossible? — It comes from the concentration of vagrant forces, from giving a direction to vague instincts, from the conventional creation of the absolute in the spheres of hope and faith!

Go on, yell at the monster, you philosophers of the eighteenth century! The monster is stronger than you are and will vanquish you. Go on, say you must crush the shameful thing, you disciples of Voltaire! But what shameful thing are you talking about? Is it the inspiring infamy of Vincent de Paul and Fénelon, the infamy which suggests so many sacrifices to the noble sisters of charity, so much devotion to the poor and chaste missionaries? A shameful thing is it, which has founded so many charitable institutions, so many refuges for the penitent, so many retreats for the innocent? If that is infamy, and if your slanders and insults are held in honour, then I embrace the pillory with all my heart and trample on your honour!

However, this was not what you were trying to say, and I will not calumniate you in my turn. Soul of Voltaire, you whom I willingly call a saintly soul, for you preferred truth and justice above all else — to you good sense was God and folly was the Devil. You only saw an ass at the cradle of Bethlehem. You saw the triumphal entry of Jesus into Jerusalem and you made fun of the ass's ears. This must have angered Fréron. Ah, if only you had lived to meet Veuillot! But we must be serious, for these are serious matters.

*The Genius of Christianity** has made its reply to the sarcasms of

---

* *Le Génie du Chritianisme*, written by Chateaubriand in 1802

Voltaire, or rather Chateaubriand has completed Voltaire, for
these two great men stand equally outside the Catholicism of the
priests.

The ass's ears are going to be indispensable as long as there are
asses in the world; and asses there will be, for nature, the
daughter of God, has placed them there.

It was the will of Jesus Christ to have an ass as His mount, and
this is why the Holy Father rides on a mule. Even his slipper is
called a mule; to indicate, perhaps, that a good pope should be
stubborn to the very nails on his toes. *Non possumus*, replied our
Holy Father, Pope Pius X, when he was asked for concessions
and reforms. The pope never says *possumus*, 'We are able', since
this is the great arcanum of the priesthood; all the priests are well
aware of it, but it is truest of all when they refrain from saying it.

The power which is founded on the mysteries must be a
mysterious power, otherwise it would no longer exist.

I believe that this man can do something which I am unable to
define because of something else which I do not understand any
more than he does. Thus I am obliged to obey him, because I
should be unable to say why I should not obey him, not being
able to deny the existence of what I do not know, the existence,
moreover, which he affirms with quite as much reason. I feel it is
irrational and am happy about it, because he tells me repeatedly
that reason is not to be trusted. I simply find that this gives me a
sense of comfort, and that I am tranquillized by this mode of
thought.

– Charbonnier, you are right.

Abortive or disappointing love affairs, frustrated ambitions,
impotent fits of anger, embittered resentments, pride which goes
before a fall, a laziness of mind which tires of doubt, the leap of
ignorance into the unknown especially when it is marvellous,
vague fears of death, the pangs of a bad conscience, the need for a
repose which constantly evades us, the sombre and grandiose
dreams of artists, dread visions of eternity: these are the forces
which religion gathers together and of which she forms the most
invincible and most formidable passion of all – devotion.

This passion is unbridled, for nothing can restrain or limit it. It
glories in its excesses, and believes that it has taken the first step
into Eternity. It absorbs all the sentiments of a man, and renders
him insensible to all else; and pushes its zeal for propaganda to

the most murderous extremes of despotism and the most implacable fury. Saint Dominic and Saint Pius V are acknowledged as such by the whole Church, and cannot be disowned by a devout and faithful Catholic.

One can understand how devotion may become a powerful lever in the hand of an authority which declares that it is infallible. 'Give me a place to stand outside the world', declared Archimedes, 'and I will move the earth.' The priests have found such a place where they can exert their pressure, beyond the pale of personal reason, and they have displaced the reason of mankind.

'Seeing that men have not attained the knowledge of God by knowledge and by reason, it has pleased us' said the Prince of Apostles, 'to save the believers by the foolishness of the faith!'

What have you to answer to this, those of you who are adversaries of the Church? Saint Paul speaks perfectly plainly here, without trying to deceive anybody.

The religious force of the dogma is in this obscurity which makes its absurdity apparent. Once a dogma has been explained, it is no longer a dogma, but a theorem in philosophy, or at least a postulate. People are always wanting to confuse religion with philosophy, and fail to understand that their separation and distinctiveness, I shall not say their antagonism, are absolutely essential to the equilibrium of reason.

Astronomers think that comets follow paths which are only relatively aberrant as far as our own system is concerned, and that they take a regular course from one system to another by describing an ellipse of which the foci are two suns.

It is the same for man's aberrant forces. A single light is insufficient for him, and to balance his progress, he needs two centres and two foci: the one is reason, and the other is faith.

CHAPTER II
The Powers of the Priests

For the priest to be powerful, he must know or he must believe. The reconciliation of science with faith is the province of the great hierophant.

If the priest knows without believing, he may be either a man of good will or a dishonest man. If he is a man of good will, he exploits the faith of others in the interests of reason and justice. If he is dishonest, he exploits their faith in the interests of his own greed, but then he is a priest no longer, he is the vilest of criminals.

If he believes without knowing, he is a respectable but dangerous dupe, who will be dominated and kept in check by the men of science.

In Christendom, priesthood and royalty are only delegations. We are all priests and kings; but since the priestly and royal functions imply the action of one man upon a multitude, we entrust our powers to a king in the temporal order, and to a priest in the spiritual order.

The Christian King is as much a priest as the rest of us, but he may not exercise his priestly office.

The Christian priest is a king like us, but he may not wield royal authority.

It is the priest's duty to guide the king, and the king's duty is to protect the priest.

The priest holds the keys and the king bears the sword. Saint Peter was the priest of early Christianity, and its king was Saint Paul.

The king and the priest hold their powers from the people as a whole, who had been consecrated king and priest by the holy unction of baptism and the application of the divine blood of Jesus Christ.

All society is safeguarded by the balance between these two powers.

If there were no pope tomorrow, there would be no king on the day after, and no person to reign either in the temporal or in the spiritual order, because no-one would obey any more; then there would be no more society and men would slaughter one another.

The pope is the priest and the priest is the pope, because the one is the representative of the other. The authority of the pope comes from the priests, and that of the priests re-ascends to the pope. Beyond that there is only God. Such, at least, is the belief of the priests.

Hence the priest disposes of divine power through those who have trust in him. I will even dare to suggest that his power has the appearance of being more than divine, because he purports to command God, and create Him at a word! Owing to the prestige attached to his person, he strips men of their pride and women of their modesty. He compels them to come and recount depravities which men would hate to be suspected of, and women would refuse to listen to outside the confessional. But once they are there it is all right to come out with their petty acts of shame, told in a low voice, and the priest pardons them or imposes a penance on them: a few prayers to say, some mortification to suffer, and they go away consoled. Is a little servitude too dear a price to pay for peace of heart?

Seeing that religion is a spiritual medicine, servitude is as certainly involved as when the doctor prescribes his remedies and submits the invalids in his care to a régime. Nobody could reasonably dispute the usefulness of medicine, but this does not justify doctors in forcing the healthy to dose and purge themselves.

It would be an amusing sight to see the president of the French Academy publish an encyclical against all those who live without laxatives, and lay under a ban those who try to do without the doctor by dint of sobriety and plenty of exercise. But the scene would change from comedy to tragedy without a hint of humour, if the government, adopting the pretensions of dean, gave the recalcitrants a straight choice between the hypodermic syringe and tyhe firing squad. The liberty of the régime is as inviolable as liberty of conscience.

You will say to me, perhaps, that one does not ask the mentally ill for their opinion before giving them cold showers. I agree, but take care: this argument could be turned against you. Those who are mad are opposed to common sense. They entertain exceptional beliefs and extravagant notions which they want to impose on others and which drive them frantic. Do not try to make us believe that the proper way to answer the defenders of the *Syllabus** is with *obligatory* cold showers.

The authority of the priest is entirely moral and cannot be imposed by force. But on the other hand, and as a fair compensation, force is unable to destroy his authority. If you kill a priest you make a martyr. Making a martyr is equivalent to laying the first stone of an altar, and every altar produces its seminaries of priests. If you knock an altar down, twenty more will be built from the scattered stones which you will not demolish a second time. Religion is no human invention, it is inevitable, that is to say providential; it comes into being of its own accord to satisfy a human need, and that is why God has willed it and revealed it.

The man in the street believes in it because it is incomprehensible to him, and apparently it is sufficiently irrational to appeal to him and win his allegiance. As for me, I believe in it because I understand it and because I should think it absurd not to believe in it.

'It is I, be not afraid,' said Christ, as he walked on the waves at the height of the storm.

'Lord, if it be thou,' said Saint Peter, 'bid me to come to you, also walking on the waves.'

'Come!' replied the Saviour, and Saint Peter walked on the sea. Suddenly the wind blew more furiously, the rollers rose and fell, and the man was afraid; immediately he began to sink, and Jesus, catching hold of him and holding him up with His hand, said to him: 'O thou of little faith, wherefore didst thou doubt?'

* Probably the Syllabus of contemporary views set out and condemned by Pius IX in 1864.

CHAPTER III
The Chaining of the Devil

Pleasure is a foe which is fated to become either our slave or our master. To possess it we must fight it, and before we can enjoy pleasure it has to be conquered.

Pleasure makes a charming slave but a cruel, pitiless and murderous master. It tires, exhausts and kills everyone it owns; after cheating all their desires and betraying all their hopes. Servitude to some pleasure is called a passion. Domination over some pleasure is called a power.

Nature has partnered pleasure with duty; if we divorce it from duty it festers and poisons us. If we devote ourselves to duty, pleasure will no longer be divorced from duty but will follow us and be our reward. Pleasure is inseparable from goodness. The upright man may suffer, it is true, but a tremendous pleasure emerges for him out of his sufferings. Job on his dunghill was visited by God who consoled and relieved him; while Nebuchadnezzar on his throne fell beneath a fatal hand which deprived him of his reason and transformed him into a beast. Jesus gave a shout of triumph as He died on the cross, as if he could feel His imminent resurrection; whereas Tiberius, in the midst of his criminal pleasures on Capri, laid bare the agonies of his soul in a letter to the Senate in which he wrote that he felt he died every day!

Evil only gets a grip on us through our vices and through the fear with which it inspires us. The Devil hunts down those who are frightened of him, and flees from those who resist him boldly. The art of chaining up demons is to do good and fear nothing.

You must not imagine that we are engaged in writing a book of morals. What we are doing is revealing secrets which magical science applies in spiritual healing. Hence it is necessary to say something about possession and exorcisms.

Each one of us can feel a dual life within ourselves. The struggle of the mind against the conscience; of unmanly desire against noble feelings; in a word, of the brute against the intelligent creature; the weakness of will so often betrayed by passion; the reproaches with which we upbraid ourselves; our self-mistrust; the dreams which haunt us in our waking hours: all this seems to demonstrate within us two persons of a different character, one of whom urges us to do good while the other tries to involve us in evil.

Owing to the natural anxieties arising from our double nature, it has been concluded that each of us is attended by two angels at all times, one good and the other evil, one on our right hand and the other on our left. This is purely and simply a piece of symbolism but, as we have said before (and this is an arcanum of the science), the human imagination is powerful enough to clothe the beings whom it affirms verbally in forms which are transiently real. More than one ascetic has engaged in hand-to-hand combat with his familiar demon.

In the visions which we have induced or which arise from a morbid disposition, we appear to ourselves under forms which lend a magnetic projection to our exalted imagination. Sometimes, too, certain people who are ill or deranged are able to project forces which magnetize the objects submitted to their action, so that these objects seem to move about of their own accord.

These productions of images and forces, since they do not belong to the usual order of nature, always emanate from some unhealthy condition which is suddenly able to become contagious by the effects of surprise, of fright or of some evil disposition.

At this stage prodigies multiply and everything seems to be caught up in a whirl of madness. Such phenomena are clearly disorders. They are the products of the evil magnetism, and the man in the street would be right, if he agrees with our definition of such beings, to call it the work of a demon.

This is the mode of production of the miracles of the convulsionaries of Saint-Médard, of the shakers of the Cévennes and of many others. Thus are produced the singular features of spiritism; people in an exalted frame of mind or in some way diseased are the focal point of all their circles, at the head of all their currents. Thanks to the action of the current and the pressure of the circles, it is possible for the sick to become incurable and for the over-excited to go mad.

When visionary exaltation and magnetic derangement are produced by an invalid's chronic condition, he is either obsessed or possessed according to the seriousness of the illness.

In this state the subject is attacked by a kind of infectious hypnotism. He dreams with his eyes open, believes in and produces irrational conditions around him, up to a certain point, and fascinates the sight and deceives the senses of impressionable folk in his vicinity. This is how superstition triumphs and the deeds of the Devil become evident. Yes, they are evident, but the Devil is not what we think. Magic could be defined as the science of universal magnetism, but this would be to take the effect for the cause. The cause, as we have said, is the ruling light of the *od*, the *ob* and the *aour* of the Hebrews. However, we must revert to the subject of magnetism, of which the great secrets are still unknown, and reveal its future theorems.

I

All beings existing in some form or other, are polarized for the purpose of inspiring and respiring the universal life.

II

The magnetic forces in the three kingdoms are composed so as to strike a balance by the power of contraries.

III

Electricity is nothing but the special heat which produces the circulation of magnetism.

IV

Medicines do not cure disease by the specific action of their substance, but through their magnetic properties.

V

Every plant is sympathetic to some animal and antipathetic to a contrary animal. Every animal is sympathetic to one man and antipathetic to another. The presence of an animal can change the character of a disease.

Many an old maid would go mad if she did not have a cat, and will be quite reasonable if she can get her cat to live on good terms with a dog.

VI

There is not a plant, insect or stone which does not conceal some magnetic property and which is not capable of serving the human will for good or ill.

VII

Man has a natural power of helping his fellow-men, by an act of will, by the spoken word, by his look and by signs. In order to exercise this power it is necessary to know and to believe in it.

VIII

Every act of will which does not express itself in a sign is an idle act. Signs may be either direct or indirect. A direct sign is stronger because it is more rational; but an indirect sign is always a sign or action corresponding to an idea, and as such it is capable of realizing the will. However, the indirect sign is only effective when the direct sign is impossible.

IX

Every decision to act is a magnetic projection. Every assent to an action serves to attract magnetism.

Every act by consent is a pact. Initially, every pact is a free engagement, afterwards it is bound by fate.

X

To act on others without binding oneself, one needs that perfect independence belonging to God alone. Can man become godlike? – Yes, by participation!

XI

To exercise great power without being perfectly free is to consign oneself to a great fatality. This is why it is scarcely possible for a sorcerer to repent and why his damnation is so sure.

XII

The power of the mage and the sorcerer is one and the same;

with this difference, the mage clings to the tree when he cuts off
the branch while the sorcerer hangs from the very branch he is
trying to cut off.

XIII

To make use of exceptional natural forces is to place oneself
outside the law. Therefore it is to submit to martyrdom if one is
just and, if one is not, to legitimate punishment.

XIV

> *De par le roi défense à Dieu*
> *De faire miracle en ce lieu.*
> (God does no wonders here you see,
> The King forbids them by decree.)

This is an inscription which is paradoxical in form only. The
police of any given place belong to the king and are his
representatives. God cannot set Himself against His own police.
He can throw evil popes and bad kings onto the dung heap, but
He cannot disregard the ruling laws. Hence every miracle which
is done in defiance of the spiritual and legal authority of the pope
or against the temporal and legal authority of the king, *does not
come from God*, but from the Devil.

God in the world means order and authority; it is Satan who
stands for disorder and anarchy. Why is it not only permissible
but even glorious to resist a tyrant? It is because the tyrant is an
anarchist who has usurped power. Do you wish to fight
victoriously against evil? Be the personification of what is good.
Do you want to conquer anarchy? Be the arm of authority. Do
you want to chain up Satan? Be the power of God.

Now, the power of God reveals itself in human beings by two
forces: collective faith and incontestable reason.

Therefore, there are two kinds of unfailing exorcisms, those of
reason and those of faith. Faith issues its commands to the
phantoms of which she is queen because she is their mother, and
they depart for a season. Reason breathes on them in the name of
science and they disappear for ever.

CHAPTER IV
The Supernatural and the Divine

The man in the street calls anything which looks to him contrary to nature, supernatural.

The contest against nature is the insane dream of the ascetics; as if nature were not the very law of God.

They have given the name concupiscence to the legitimate allurements of nature. They have fought against sleep, against hunger and thirst, and against sexual desire. They have fought not simply to secure the triumph of superior attractions, but with the thought in mind that nature is corrupt and that the satisfaction of nature is an evil. The result has been strange aberrations. Insomnia has created delirium, fasting has eaten into the brain and filled it with phantoms, forced celibacy has given new life to monstrous impurities.

Incubi and succubi have infested the cloisters. Priapism and hysteria have always created a life of hell for monks with no vocation and for presumptuous nuns.

Saint Anthony and Saint Theresa struggled against lewd phantoms; in their imaginations they attended orgies of which ancient Babylon had no conception.

Marie Alacoque and Messalina suffered the same torments: those of a desire which has become exalted above nature and is impossible to satisfy.

At the same time, there is this difference between them, that if Messalina had been able to foresee Marie Alacoque, she would have envied her.

To see all men combined into a single individual, as Caligula would have wished in his thirst for blood, and to see this man of men open his breast and give her his bleeding and burning heart to dote on, and to dote on it as consolation for never being sated with love, what a dream that would have been for Messalina!

Love, that triumph of nature, cannot be ravished by her
without her being indignant. When it imagines it has become
supernatural its condition is unnatural and the most monstrous of
impurities is that which profanes and prostitutes the idea of God
in some way. Ixion, when he assaulted Juno and spent his virile
strength on a naked female avenger, was, in the high symbolic
philosophy of the ancients, the type of this sacrilegious passion
punished in Tartarus by serpent fetters which bound him to an
ever-whirling wheel. Erotic passion, when deflected from its
legitimate object and raised to a foolish desire to commit some
sort of violence on the infinite, is the wildest of mental
aberrations, and like the madness of the Marquis de Sade it thirsts
for tortures and blood. The young girl lacerates her breasts with
metal underwear, the exhausted man, misled by fastings and
vigils, abandons himself completely to the depraved pleasures of a
flagellation which is full of strange sensations, and then will fall
worn out into hours of sleep filled with enervating dreams.

Diseases which are the despair of science will result from
excesses like these. All the senses will lose their natural uses to
assist illusory sensations; stigmata, more frightful than the sores of
syphilis, will etch wounds in the hands and feet and around the
head which ooze intermittently and are extremely painful. Soon
the victim will no longer see, hear or take nourishment, and will
remain plunged in a deep state of idiocy from which he will only
emerge to die, unless a terrible reaction of hysteria and priapism
occurs which will look like the direct action of a demon.

Woe, then, to Urbain Grandier and Gaufridi! The fury of the
bacchantes who tore Orpheus to pieces will seem like innocent
games compared to the frenzy of the pious doves of the Lord
given over to the rage of sexual passion!

Who will tell us the indescribable romances of the Carthusian's
cell or of the lonely pallet where the cloistered monk appears to
sleep? The jealousies of the divine spouse, his acts of neglect
which drive one to madness, his caresses which bring a thirst for
love! The repulses of the succubus who is crowned with stars!
The scornful looks of the Virgin, queen of the angels, the
kindnesses of Jesus Christ!

Oh! the lips which have once drunk from this fatal cup remain
parched and trembling. Hearts once fired by this delirium find
the true sources of love dry and insipid. What is a man to a

woman who has had dreams of a God? What is woman to the
man whose heart has thrilled to the eternal beauty? Ah! poor,
mad creatures, they no longer mean anything to you although
they are everything; for they are reality, reason and life.

Your dreams are only dreams, your phantoms are only
phantoms. God, the living law, God, the supreme wisdom, is in
no way an accomplice of your follies nor the possible object of
your hopeless passions; a bristle which has dropped from a man's
beard, a single hair lost by a woman of flesh and blood are things
much better and more positive than your consuming fancies.
Give your sexual love to one another and let God have your
adoration.

The true worship of God is not the prostration of man in a
blind delirium; on the contrary, it is calm exaltation in reason
and light. The true love of God is not Saint Anthony's
nightmare; on the contrary it is profound peace, the tranquillity
which arises from perfect order. Everything that man thinks of as
supernatural in his own life is anti-natural, and whatever is anti-
natural is an offence to God. This is something of which a true
sage should be well aware!

There is nothing supernatural, not even God, as nature shows.
Nature is His law, His thought. Nature is Himself and if He
could give the lie to nature He would be able to make an attempt
on His own existence. The alleged divine miracle, if it emanated
from the eternal order, would be the suicide of God.

A man may naturally heal others since Jesus Christ did it;
saints and magnetizers have done it and are doing it every day. A
man can rise from the earth, walk on the water, etc.; he can do
everything that Jesus was able to do, who Himself said: 'Those
who believe will do the works I do, and even greater works than
these.'

Jesus resuscitated the dead, but He never evoked their souls. In
resuscitating a man one relieves the lethargy which usually
precedes death. Evoking after death imparts a retrograde
movement to life; it does violence to nature, which Jesus could
not do.

The divine miracle is nature when it obeys reason; the infernal
miracle is nature when it seems to fall into confusion so as to
obey folly. The true miracle is human life, good sense, patient
and tranquil reason, the wisdom which can believe without peril

because it can manage to doubt without rancour or anger; it is persistent goodwill which seeks, which studies, which waits. It is Rabelais, the man who praised wine, often drank water, performed all the duties of a good parish priest and wrote his *Pantagruel*. One day, when Jean de La Fontaine had put his socks on inside out he solemnly asked whether Saint Augustine had as much sense as Rabelais. Put your socks on the right way, friend La Fontaine, and take care not to ask such questions in future; perhaps de Fontenelle is shrewd enough to understand you, but he is certainly not bold enough to answer you.

Not everything we imagine is God is God, and not everything we imagine is the Devil is the Devil.

What is divine baffles human appreciation, especially when it comes to ordinary men. Beauty is always simple, truth appears commonplace, and what is just escapes notice because nobody is shocked by it. Order is never observed; it is disorder which attracts attention because it is awkward and intrusive. Small children are insensible to harmony, for the most part, they prefer uproar and noise; exactly so, in life, many people look for drama and romance. They despise the beautiful sun and dream about the splendours of the lightning, they imagine that virtue goes with hemlock and Cato might have lived free; but if they had been true sages, would the world have recognized them?

Saint Martin, who gave the name 'unknown philosopher' to the initiates of true wisdom, did not believe it. To keep silent is one of the great laws of occultism. Now, to keep silent is to hide oneself. God is the all-powerful who conceals Himself, and Satan is the egotistical lack of power who is always trying to display himself.

CHAPTER V
Sacred Rites and Accursed Rites

The Bible relates how two priests who had put profane fire in their censers were consumed as they stood before the altar by a jealous explosion of holy fire. This story is a warning allegory.

To tell the truth, rites are neither indifferent nor arbitrary. Efficacious rites are those which are consecrated by the legitimate authority. Sacrilegious rites always produce an effect which is contrary to that intended by the rash operator.

The rites of the ancient religions, superseded and annulled by Christianity, are profane and accursed rites for those who have no serious belief in those religions now outlawed.

Neither Judaism nor the other great faiths of the East have yet said their last word. They are condemned but not yet judged; and until judgement has been passed their declarations may be treated as legitimate.

Those rites which have been left behind in the march of religious progress are profane and to a certain extent accursed by this very token. The time will come when grandeurs in the Judaic dogma which are still unknown will be opened to the understanding, but this will not mean that the Christian world will revert to circumcision.

The Samaritan schism was a return to the symbolism of Egypt, and nothing remains of it. The ten tribes have disappeared, to be mingled with the gentiles and absorbed by them for ever.

The rites of the Hebrew grimoires, already condemned by the Law of Moses, belong to the worship of the patriarchs who sacrificed victims on the mountains in the process of evoking visions. It is a crime to want to go back to the sacrifice of Abraham.

The Catholic and Orthodox Christians alone have established a doctrine and set up a form of worship; the heretics and sectarians have been able to do no more than deny, suppress and destroy. They conduct us in the direction of a vague deism and the negation of all revealed religion. In other words they relegate God to such deep obscurity that people are hardly interested to know whether He really exists any more.

Outside the authoritative and positive affirmations of Moses and Jesus Christ concerning the Godhead, there are only doubts, hypotheses and fantasies.

For those ancient races who hated the Jews and whom the Jews detested, God was nothing more than the Spirit of Nature, gracious as the spring and terrible as the tempest; and the thousand transformations of this protean being peopled the various pantheons of the world with a great multitude of gods.

But above all reigned Destiny, or Fate. The gods of the ancients were only natural forces. Nature herself was the great Panthea. The fatal consequences of such a dogma were inevitably materialism and slavery.

The God of Moses and of Jesus Christ is One. He is spirit; He is eternal, independent, immutable and infinite; He can do all things, He has created all things and He rules all things. He has made man in His own image and likeness. He is our only Father and our only Master. The consequences of these doctrines are spirituality and liberty.

Unfortunately, an antagonism between the things themselves has been understood on the basis of this antagonism between ideas. Pantheism has been made out to be an enemy of God, as if pantheism had any real existence other than in God's own empire. Nature has been set up as a power in revolt; love has been called Satan; matter has been given a spirit which it cannot possibly have and, by the fatalistic law of equilibrium, the result has been to make religious doctrines materialistic. A misconception has arisen from this conflict, or should we say a vast misunderstanding: it is that man has recovered his freedom in the name of the fatalism which fetters him and is enslaved in the name of God who alone is able and desires to set him free. The outcome of this perversity of judgment is an incredible malaise and a sort of moral paralysis because one can see dangers at every turn.

You may take my word for it that I have not the slightest inclination to choose between Proudhon and Veuillot.

Dead religions never revive, and as Jesus Christ has said, a man does not put new wine in old bottles. When the rites become ineffectual the priesthood disappears. Nevertheless, the secret rites of the universal religion are preserved through all the religious changes, and it is in the rationale and value of these rites that the great secret of Freemasonry consists.

In fact, the masonic symbols in their totality constitute a religious synthesis which is still missed by the Roman Catholic priesthood. Count Joseph de Maistre felt this instinctively; and when, fearing to see the world without religion, he aspired after a close alliance between science and faith, he involuntarily turned his eyes towards the half-open doors of occultism.

Today, masonic occultism no longer exists, and the portals of initiation have been flung wide open. All has been divulged, all has been written down. The *Tiler* and the masonic rituals are on sale for anyone to buy. The Grand-Orient has no more mysteries, or at least no more for the layman than for the initiates; but the masonic rites still trouble the heart of Rome, because she feels they have some power in them which escapes her.

This power is the liberty of the human conscience, it is the independent essential ethics of every cult. It is the right not to be damned or consigned to eternal death because one does without the ministrations of the priests; a ministration which is only necessary for those who feel the need for it, respectable for everybody when it is offered without imposition, horrible when it is abused.

The ban of the Church strengthens its enemies. Unjust excommunication is a sort of hallowing. Jacques de Molay, burnt at the stake, was the judge of the pope and the king. Savonarola, burnt by Alexander VI, was then the venerable vicar and representative of Jesus Christ; and when he refused the sacraments to the bogus Jansenists, the deacon Pâris performed miracles.

Two kinds of rites, therefore, can be efficacious in magic: sacred rites and accursed rites, since malediction is a negative consecration. Exorcism makes possession, and when the infallible Church endeavours to chase the Devil away she goes some way towards creating him.

The Roman Catholic Church exactly reproduces the image of God as He has been depicted with so much genius by the authors of the *Siphra Dzeniûta*, expounded by Rabbi Simeon and his disciples. She has two faces, one of light, the other of shade, and as far as she is concerned harmony results from the analogy of contraries. The face of light is the gentle and smiling countenance of Mary. The dark face is the grimace of the demon. I dare to tell the demon quite openly what I think of his grimace, and I do not think this will offend the Church my mother. If perchance she condemns my temerity; if the decision of some future council declares the personal existence of the Devil, I shall bow to it on the strength of my principles themselves. I have stated that the word creates what it affirms; now, the Church is the depositary of the authority of the word; at such time as it affirms not only the real but the personal existence of the Devil, the Devil will personally exist, the Roman Church having created him.

The madonnas who do miracles always have black faces, because the general populace loves to look on the dark side of religion. The same applies to doctrines as to contrasty pictures: if you reduce the shadows you weaken the highlights.

It is necessary to re-establish in the Church the priesthood of illumination in place of the priesthood of temporal influence. It is necessary for the clergy to be taught science, for the deep study of nature to redress and direct exegesis. It is necessary for the priests to be mature men, who have proved themselves in the battles of life; for the bishops to be superior to the priests in wisdom and virtue; for the pope to be more learned and wise than the bishops. It is necessary that the priests should be elected by the laity, the bishops by the priests and the pope by the bishops. It is necessary that there should be a progressive initiation into the priesthood, that the occult sciences should be studied by the candidates for the sacred ministry, above all that great Jewish Qabalah which is the key to all symbology. Only thus will the true universal religion be revealed, and the Catholicism of all ages and peoples replace the present absurd and odious Catholicism which is the enemy of progress and liberty, which still fights in the world against truth and justice, but whose reign has already passed away for ever.

In the present-day Church, as in Judaism during the days of Jesus Christ, tares are mixed in with the good corn, and one dare not touch the tares for fear of rooting out the wheat. The Church is being punished by her own anathemas; she *is* cursed because she *has* cursed. The sword she has drawn has turned against her, just as the Master predicted.

Maledictions belong to hell and anathemas are the acts of the popery of Satan. They should be shut up again in the grimoire of Honorius. The true Church of God prays for sinners and has no care for cursing them.

Fathers are censured who curse their children, but no-one has been found to admit that a mother might have cursed hers. The rites of excommunication used in barbaric times were those of sympathetic, or black, magic, as it proved by the fact that the holy things were veiled and all the lights were extinguished to render homage to darkness. Then the populaces were incited to rebel against their kings, extermination and hatred were preached, whole realms were interdicted, and the magnetic current of evil was strengthened by all possible means. This current has become a powerful vortex which is shaking the Chair of Peter, but the Church will triumph by indulgence and pardon. A day will come when the last anathemas of an oecumenical council will be these: Accursed be malediction, let anathemas be anathematized, and may all men be blessed! − Then we shall no longer see mankind on one side and the Church on the other; for the Church will embrace mankind, and whoever is included in humanity cannot be otherwise than within the pale of the Church.

Dissident doctrines will only be regarded as ignorance. Love will do gentle violence to hatred, and we shall remain united by all the sentiments of sincere brotherhood, even with those who would wish to separate themselves from us. At that time religion will have conquered the world, and the Jews, our fathers and brothers, will join us in greeting the spiritual reign of the Messiah. This is the future prospect for our earth, which is now so desolate and unhappy: the second coming of the Saviour, the manifestation of grand Catholicism and the triumph of Messianism, our hope and our faith! ...

CHAPTER VI
Concerning Divination

Divination may be carried out in two ways: by sagacity or by second sight.

Sagacity is the accurate observation of facts together with the legitimate inference of effects and causes.

Second sight is a special intuition, comparable to that exhibited by clairvoyants who read the past, present and future in the universal light. Edgar Allan Poe, a clairvoyant on artificial stimulants, wrote in his *Tales* about a certain Auguste Dupin who read thoughts and unravelled the mysteries of the most tangled affairs by using a very special system of observations and deductions.

It would be all to the good if examining magistrates were thoroughly initiated into August Dupin's system.

Quite often, clues which are neglected as insignificant would lead to the truth being discovered if they were followed up. At times this truth would be strange, unexpected and almost unbelievable, as in Poe's tale, *The Murders in The Rue Morgue*. What would be said, for instance, if it came out that no-one was really responsible for the poisoning of Mr Lafarge, that it was perpetrated by a sleep-walker who, impelled by vague fears (if she were a woman), went furtively in her sleep, while in a deceptive clairvoyant state, to make a substitution, to mix the arsenic, baking powder and powdered gum in Marie Capelle's boxes, believing in her dream that this would prevent the poisoning she might have feared for her son?

Of course we are advancing an inadmissible hypothesis here, after the verdict of guilty, but one which, before the verdict, might have been worth careful examination in the light of the following facts:

1. Mrs Lafarge, the mother, kept on talking about poisoning and mistrusted her daughter-in-law who, in an unfortunate letter, boasted about possessing arsenic;
2. The same lady never undressed and even slept in her shawl;
3. Some extraordinary noises were heard at night in this old Grandier house;
4. The arsenic was scattered everywhere throughout the house, on the furniture, in the drawers, on the fabrics, in a way which excluded all intelligence and reason;
5. There was arsenic mixed with the powdered gum in a box which Marie Capelle herself sent to her young friend Emma Pontier, as containing the gum she used for herself and which she admitted having mixed in Mr Lafarge's drinks.

Such singular circumstances would have undoubtedly exercised the sagacity of August Dupin or of Zadig, but made no impression whatsoever on the jurors and judges mortally biased against the accused by the wretched evidence of the theft of the diamonds. So she was condemned quite fairly, for justice is always in the right; but we do know with what energy the unhappy woman protested right up to her death, and what reputable sympathizers she had around her until her final moments.

Another convicted person, less attractive no doubt, also protested his innocence at the bar of religion and his fellow men up to the dread moment of death. He was the unhappy Léotade, accused and found guilty of the murder and rape of a child. Edgar Allan Poe could have based one of his gripping tales on this tragic report. He would have altered the names of those involved and set the scene in England or America, and might have put these words into the mouth of Auguste Dupin:

The child went into the educational establishment, from which she was not seen to emerge. The porter, who always locked the door with a key, was only away for a moment. When he came back the child was no longer there, but she had left the door open.

The unfortunate infant was discovered the following day in the cemetery, near to the wall of the boarding-school. She was dead, and appeared to have been battered by someone's fists, her ears were torn, and she bore the marks of a completely abnormal sexual assault: her injuries were frightful to see. There were no other special features such as would accompany a rape carried out by a man.

In addition to this she did not look as if she had fallen where she lay, but as if she had been put there. Her clothes were wrapped under and around her. She was dry, although it had been raining all night; she must have been brought there in a sack just before dawn, either through the gate or through a gap in the graveyard wall. Her garments were soiled by matter passed from the bowels, in which they appeared to have been rolled.

This is what must have happened. The little girl, on entering the parlour, suddenly needed to go to the toilet; accordingly she slipped outside by the door which had been left open, and as fate would have it was seen by nobody.

She looked for some dark alley next to the cemetery, and there she was pounced on by some evil woman whose doorway she might often have soiled, and who was on the watch, having sworn to give a severe beating to any boy or girl she could catch.

This person threw her door open suddenly, started punching the child and bruised her face, pulled her ears half off, and rolled her in her own excreta. Then she saw that the hapless child no longer stirred. She had only wanted to beat her and had killed her.

What was she going to do with the corpse, or what she thought was a corpse, for the poor girl may have been stunned rather than dead? She hid the body in a sack, went out, and then overheard someone say that they were looking for a young boarder who had gone into the school but had not been seen to leave.

She was seized by a horrible idea: suspicion had to be diverted from her at all costs; the victim must be found at the foot of the school wall and look as if she had been raped, making it impossible to blame the crime on a woman.

So the assault was simulated by means of a stick, and it may be that the unfortunate child died during this last atrocity.

After night had fallen, the crone carried the sack into the cemetery, using a knife-blade to force the lock of its badly shut gate. She took the precaution of walking out backwards, obliterating her footprints as she went, and carefully shut the gate again.

This is the only hypothesis, according to Dupin, which can explain all the seemingly inexplicable circumstances in this dreadful story.

In fact, if the bursar of the school had violated the little girl he would have tried to smother her screams not to provoke them by pulling her ears violently and bruising her with blows. If she had cried out, her cries would have been heard, for the store-room, which was pointed out as the only possible place for the crime inside the house, contains windows overlooking a barracks full of soldiers and almost on a level with the sentry-box.

Not only so, but the accused was seen throughout the day, quietly performing his duties. Even his colleagues supported his alibi for the hour of the crime; but owing to one or two discrepancies and equivocations, they were accused of complicity or at the very least partiality, and it is therefore likely that he will be found guilty by the Philadelphia court.

So says Auguste Dupin in the 'unpublished tale by Poe' which we have imagined he might have written; a liberty we think we shall be allowed to take in order to offer our hypothesis without bringing ourselves into contempt of court.

We know how Solomon was wise enough to tell in an infallible manner who was the real mother of a child claimed by two women.

The study of physiognomy, bearing and habits is another sure way of telling a man's secret thoughts and character. The shapes of head and hand also provide valuable pointers for induction; but account must always be taken of the free human will, which can successfully counter evil inclinations natural to man.

It should also be borne in mind that someone who is naturally good can become depraved, and that often the best turn out to be the worst when they allow themselves to be degraded and corrupted. A knowledge of the great and infallible laws of equilibrium can help us here to predict the destiny of men. A nonentity or mediocre man will be able to attain everything and will never amount to nothing. A sensual man who throws himself into his excesses will perish in these same excesses, or else will be forced back into a contrary form of excess. The Christianity of the stylites and the desert fathers was inevitable after the debaucheries of Tiberius and Heliogabalus. In the heyday of Jansenism the ground was laid, exactly in that terrible form of Christianity whose folly is an outrage to nature, for the orgies of the Regency and the Directory. The excesses of liberty in '93 called forth despotism. The exaggeration of any force always turns to the advantage of the contrary force.

This is why, in philosophy and in religion, exaggerated truths become the most dangerous untruths. When, for example, Jesus Christ said to His apostles: 'Whoever hears you hears me, and he who listens to me pays attention to Him who sent me', He established a disciplined priesthood and unity of teaching; attributing by this method, which is divine because it is natural, a relative infallibility to those whom He Himself had taught, but not giving any ecclesiastical tribunal on this account the right to condemn the discoveries of Galileo. Exaggerations of the principle of doctrinal and disciplinary infallibility have led to the Church being caught red-handed persecuting the truth. The Church seems unmindful of the rights of reason; the rights of faith have been unrecognized by others. The human spirit is a cripple walking on two crutches: science and religion. False philosophy has taken away its religion and fanaticism has snatched away its science. What can it do? It can only fall heavily to the ground, and drag itself along legless between the blasphemies of Proudhon and the blunders of the *Syllabus*.

The madness of unbelief is no match for the frenzy of fanaticism, because it is ridiculous. Fanaticism is an exaggerated affirmation and unbelief an equally exaggerated negation, but most laughably so. For what is really the exaggeration of nothing? Much less than nothing! Hardly a matter for breaking lances over.

Thus impotence and discouragement on the one hand, and persistence and encroachment on the other, cause us to sink under the heavy weight of blind beliefs and of the interests which exploit them. The old world we thought was dead stands up again in front of us and the revolution has to begin all over again.

All this could have been written down − all this was written down in the law of equilibrium; all this has been predicted, and one could easily go on to predict what will happen next.

The revolutionary spirit is now agitating and tormenting those nations which have remained absolutely Catholic: Italy, Spain and Ireland; and the Catholic reaction, in the sense of exaggeration and despotism, hovers over the nations tired of revolutions. While this is going on, Protestant Germany grows greater and places a formidable temporal power at the service of liberty of conscience and independence of thought.

France puts its Voltairian sword at the disposal of clerical reaction, and so encourages the development of materialism. Religion is being turned into a policy and an industry. The best minds are deserting her and taking refuge in science; but, as it goes deeper into the analysis of matter, science will end up by finding God and will compel religion to come to her. The theological absurdities of the Middle Ages will become so obviously impossible, that it will be thought foolish even to contend against them. At that time, the letter will give place to the spirit and the great universal religion will be known by the world for the first time.

No divination of the future is involved in predicting this great movement, for it has already begun and its effects are already manifesting themselves in its causes. Every day new discoveries are throwing light on the obscure texts of Genesis and vindicate the old fathers of the Qabalah. Camille Flammarion has already shown us God in the Universe; those voices which condemned Galileo have been reduced to silence long since, and nature which suffered calumny for such a length of time now justifies herself as we get to know her better. Vanini's piece of straw knew more about the existence of God than all the schoolmen, and the blasphemers of yesterday are the prophets of tomorrow.

That other creations may have preceded our own, that the days of Genesis may be periods of years or even periods of centuries, that the sun arrested in its course by Joshua may be part of a piece of oriental poetic imagery, that things which would be absurd as history may be interpreted as allegories, does not in any way harm the majesty of the Bible or contradict its authority at all.

Everything in this holy book which is doctrinal or moral comes under the jurisdiction of the Church; but all matters of archaeology, chronology, physics or history etc., belong exclusively to science, of which the authority in such things is completely distinct from, if not independent of, that pertaining to faith.

This has already been recognized by the most enlightened priests, although they have not dared to say so openly; and they are right to keep silent. One would not wish the leaders of the caravan to march more quickly than the old people and little children. Those who were too encumbered to push themselves to the front would soon be left behind and would perish in their isolation, as happened to Lamennais and to so many others. It is essential to be well briefed on the route back to the camp, and to be always ready to return at the least alarm, to avoid being charged with negligence when scouting ahead.

After the advent of the Messianic age, that is to say when the reign of Christ has been set up on earth, wars will cease, because politics will no longer consist of the double-dealing of the most artful or the bullying tactics of the strongest. Indeed, there will be one international law, for international obligation will be universally proclaimed and recognized. Then, and then only, shall Christ's prediction come to pass: 'There shall be one fold and One Shepherd.'

If all the Protestant sects were to join together and rally to the Greek Orthodox Church, acknowledging as pope the spiritual head whose see would be at Constantinople, there would be two Roman Catholic Churches in the world; because Constantinople was once, and will yet again be, the new Rome. Schism would then only have a very short life. A truly oecumenical council, made up of deputies from the whole Christian world, would put an end to disagreement as was done once before at the time of the Council of Constance. And the world would be amazed to find itself entirely Catholic; but this time with that liberty of conscience which has been won by the Protestants, and the right to an independent ethic demanded by the philosophers: nobody being obliged under legal penalties to use the remedies of religion, and nobody being allowed to deny the grandeurs of the faith or to insult science, which is the foundation of philosophy, as is no less reasonable.

That is what the philosophy of wisdom, of which Paracelsus spoke, clearly shows us for the future; and we have had little trouble in reaching this divination by a series of deductions which start from actual facts which are happening under our eyes.

These things will occur sooner or later and it will be the triumph of order; but the march of events which will lead up to them can be held up by sanguinary catastrophes ceaselessly prepared and fomented by the revolutionary spirit. This spirit is often inspired by a fierce thirst for justice and is capable of the utmost heroism and devotion, but it is always deceived, debased and set off course by the magnetism of evil.

Besides, if one is to believe the prophetic tradition, perfect order will not rule the earth before the last judgement, that is to say before the transformation and renovation of our planet. Faulty or fallen men are the enemies of truth and incapable of any other motive, for the most part. They are separated by their vanity and greed, always separated; and according to the prophets from apostolic times to the present day, justice will not reign perfectly on the earth until the wicked have either been converted or suppressed, and Christ, accompanied by His angels and saints, descends from Heaven to be king.

There are causes which human wisdom cannot foresee, which give rise to vast events.

The invention of a new gun alters the balance of power in Europe, and Mr Thiers, that clever but unprincipled man, considering that politics consists of loading the dice, joined forces with Veuillot on the cart of Juggernaut, in what could be called the temporal papacy. Did Jesus foresee all this? Yes, perhaps during His agony in the Garden of Gethsemane and certainly afterwards when he made this terrible prediction to Saint Peter: 'Those who take the sword must perish by the sword.'

Possibly it will take a martyr pope to re-establish a truly Christian papacy in the legitimate exercise of its double power! Count Joseph de Maistre said that torture makes supplication, and when the earth has been parched by the arid breath of irreligion it will call for showers of blood.

The blood of the guilty is purified when it is shed, because Jesus, in allowing Himself to be hanged on the cross, sanctified all the instruments of torture; but only the blood of the just has an expiatory virtue.

The blood of Louis XVI and of Lady Elisabeth prayed in advance that supreme justice would not ignore that of Robespierre.

Divination of the future by wisdom and induction may be termed prescience. Divination by second sight or by magnetic intuition is nothing more than a presentiment. The presentimental faculty may be heightened by inducing in oneself a kind of trance with the aid of certain conventional or arbitrary signs, which immerse the train of thought into a half-waking state. These signs are drawn by lot, because it is the oracles of fate rather than those of reason which are then consulted. This is an invocation to darkness, an appeal to insanity, the sacrifice of lucid thought to the nameless entity which goes prowling in the night.

Divination, as its name indicates, is above all else a divine work, and perfect prescience can only be attributed to God. It is for this reason that men of God are naturally prophets. The good and upright man thinks and acts in union with the divinity which dwells within us all and is always speaking to us; but for most of us the clamour of our passions prevents us from hearing His voice.

The just, having brought peace to their souls, always hear this sovereign and peaceable voice, their thoughts are like a pure and level sheet of water in which the divine sun is reflected in all its splendour.

The souls of the saints are like detectors of purity; they quiver at the least irreverent contact and turn with horror from everything unclean. They have a special gift for discerning and analysing in some way the emanations from people's consciences. The malevolent make them ill at ease and the ungodly make them sad. They can see a black aura around the wicked which repels them, and a bright one around good souls which wins their heart at once. That is how Saint Germain d'Auxerre read the character of Saint Geneviève. That is how Postel found renewed youth in the society of Mother Jeanne. That is how Fénelon came to know and love the gentle, patient Madam Guyon. Vianney, the worthy parish priest of Ars, saw through the stratagems of those who approached him and it was impossible to lie to him with any success. We know that he subjected the shepherd-lads of la Salette to a severe interrogation and made them confess that they had seen nothing out-of-the-way but had entertained themselves by adapting and enlarging on an ordinary dream. There is also a type of divination which belongs to rapture and great inflamed passions.

These powers of the mind seem to create the thing they announce. Theirs is the efficacy of prayer. They say, Amen! So be it! and it is just as they have willed.

CHAPTER VII
The Point of Balance

The whole power of magic is in the central point of the universal equilibrium.

The wisdom which strikes this equilibrium is contained in these four dicta: know the truth, will what is good, love beauty, do what is just! Because truth, goodness, beauty and justice are inseparable; so that he who knows the truth must needs will what is good, to love it because it is beautiful and to do it because it is just.

The central point in the intellectual and moral order is the link between science and faith. In human nature this central point is the medium in which soul and body combine to establish the identity of their action.

In physics it stands for the resultant of opposing forces compensated by one another.

Understand this link, take possession of this medium, act upon this resultant!

ET ERITIS SICUT DII SCIENTES BONUM ET MALUM.

('And ye shall be as gods, knowing good and evil').

The point of balance between life and death is the great secret of immortality.

The point of balance between day and night is the mainspring of the movement of the worlds.

The balancing point between science and faith is the great secret of philosophy.

The balancing point between order and liberty is the great secret of politics.

The balancing point between men and woman is the great secret of love.

The balancing point between will and emotion, between action and reaction is the great secret of power.

The great secret of high magic, the inexpressible, incommunicable secret is nothing other than the balancing point between the relative and the absolute. It is the infinity of the finite and the finite of the infinite. It is the relative almightiness of man balancing the impossibilities of God.

At this point, those who know will understand and the others will use *divination* to look for the meaning.

QUI AUTEM DIVINABUNT DIVINI ERANT.

('But those who are going to divine are already divine').

The balancing point is the essential monad which constitutes the divinity of God, liberty in the individual and harmony in nature.

In dynamics it is perpetual motion; in geometry it is squaring the circle; in chemistry it is the practical achievement of the great work.

On reaching this point angels can fly without the need of wings, and men can attain any reasonable desire.

We have just said that it is attained by the equilibrating wisdom which may be summed up in four words: to know, to will, to love, and to do what is true, good, beautiful and just.

This wisdom is the vocation of all men, because God has given to all an intelligence with which they may know, a will with which they may resolve, a heart with which they may love, and a power with which they may act.

The exercise of the intelligence applied to the truth leads to knowledge.

The exercise of the intelligence applied to what is good gives that consciousness of beauty which produces faith.

That which is false corrupts knowledge; that which is evil corrupts the will; that which is ugly corrupts love; that which is unjust cancels and perverts action. Whatever is true must be lovely; whatever is lovely must be true; what is good is always just.

The evil, the false, the ugly and the unjust are incompatible with truth.

I believe in religion because it is beautiful and because it teaches goodness. To my mind it is right to believe in it and I do not believe in the Devil because he is ugly and because he delivers us to evil and instructs us in the lie.

If anyone talks to me of a God who misleads our intelligence, stifles our reason, and wishes to torture His creatures for ever, even if they *are* blameworthy, I regard this as an ugly idea, a wicked fabrication, and would consider this almighty torturer to be supremely unjust; and by a process of rigorous reasoning I conclude that all this is false, that this so-called god has been made in the image and likeness of the devil, and I have no wish to believe in him since I do not believe in Satan.

But here I seem to be contradicting myself. The things I declare to be unjust, to be pieces of ugliness and in consequence falsities, follow from the teachings of a Church whose doctrines I profess to acknowledge and whose symbols I profess to respect.

Yes, of course, they do follow from her teachings when misunderstood, and this is why we are making appeal from the face of darkness to the head of light; from the letter to the spirit; from the theologians to the councils; from the commentators to the sacred texts; and stand in readiness to submit to lawful condemnation if we said anything over which we should have kept silence. Let it be well understood that we are not writing for the profane masses, but for the instructed of a later age than ours and for the pontiffs of the future.

Those who will prepare themselves to know the truth will also dare to will what is good; so they will love what is beautiful and will no longer take people like Veuillot as representatives of their ideals and their thoughts. From the time that a pope who is so inclined feels the force of doing only that which is just, he will no longer have to say *non possumus*, for he will be able to do anything he likes and will once more become the monarch, not simply of Rome, but of the world.

What does it matter if Peter's vessel is tossed by the tempest, has not Jesus Christ taught this prince of apostles how to walk on the waves? If he sinks it is because he is afraid, and if he is afraid it is because he has doubted his divine Master. The Saviour's hand will be stretched out, will catch hold of him and will help him to the shore. 'O man of little faith, wherefore didst thou doubt?'

Can the Church ever be in danger as far as the true believer is concerned? It is not the building itself which is shaky, it is the heterogeneous constructions with which it has been overlaid by the ignorance of the ages.

A good priest told us one day of how, on visiting a Carmelite convent, he was allowed to see an old frock said to have

belonged to the sainted founder of the order, and of how
surprised he was to see it so filthy. The nun who showed it to
him clasped her hands and exclaimed: 'This is the dirt of our holy
mother!' The priest thought, as we do, that it would have been
more respectful to wash the garment. The body dirt could not
possibly be a relic, otherwise things would have to be taken to
their logical conclusion and soon the Christians, in their
stercoraceous acts of adoration, would no longer have any
reproofs for the fetishists of the Grand Lama.

What is not beautiful is not good; what is not good is not just;
what is not just is not true.

When Voltaire, that over-enthusiastic friend of justice, chanted
his rallying cry – 'Crush the Beast!' – do you think he intended
the Gospel or its adorable Author? Was he thinking of attacking
the religion of Saint Vincent de Paul and Fénelon? No, of course
not, he was rightly indignant at the follies, the incredible
stupidities and the impious persecutions with which the quarrels
of Jansenism and Molinism filled the Church of his times. For
him, as for us, distorted religion was an infamy, an impiety
which is the worst of all impieties.

Also, when he had done his work, when the revolution had
proclaimed in accordance with the Gospel and in spite of the
interested parties: 'liberty of conscience, equality before the law
and the brotherhood of man', Chateaubriand made his
appearance and showed how to the spirit religion was beautiful,
and the world of Voltaire, having been rectified by the
Revolution, was once again ready to recognize that religion was
true.

Yes, beautiful religion is true religion and ugly religion is
untrue. Yes, it is true, the religion of Christ the consoler, of the
Good Shepherd carrying the lost sheep on His shoulders, of the
immaculate virgin, the nurse and restorer of sinners; it is true, the
religion which adopts orphans, which embraces the criminal at
the foot of the scaffold; which welcomes the poor as well as the
rich, the servant as well as the master, to the table of God, and
coloured men side-by-side with the white. It is true, the religion
which orders the sovereign pontiff to be the servant of the
servants of God, and the bishops to wash the feet of beggars!

But the religion of those who trade in the sanctuary, which
compels Peter's successor to kill in order to eat, the rancorous and

commonplace religion of Veuillot, the religion professed by the enemies of science and progress, this is false because it is ugly, because it opposes itself to what is good and favours injustice. Let us take care not to say that these mutually contradictory religions are the same. It would be like saying that polished iron or dross are silver or gold and that leprosy is the same thing as normal skin.

There is a need for religion in man: it is an incontestable fact which science is compelled to recognize; this need is felt by a special inner sense: the sense of eternity and infinity. Some emotions when once experienced are never forgotten: those of devotion.

The Brahmin discovers them when lost in the contemplation of Iswara; the Israelite is possessed by them in the presence of Adonai; the devout Catholic nun sheds tears of love on the feet of her crucifix. Do not try to tell them these are illusions and lies: they would give you a pitying smile, and rightly so. Each of them has been filled with beams of light from the Eternal Thought. They behold it; and the feelings they must experience in the presence of those who deny are the feelings of sighted people who hear a blind man deny the existence of the sun.

So faith has its own evidence. Now here we have a truth the knowledge of which is indispensable: a man without faith is incomplete; he lacks the first of all the interior senses. Morals will be limited for him of necessity and will amount to very little. It is possible for morals to be independent of this or that dogma, of the prescriptions of this or that priest; but they cannot exist without the religious sentiment, because without that sentiment human dignity becomes a matter of dispute or quite arbitrary. Lacking God and the immortality of the soul, what is the best, the most loving and the most faithful of men? He is a talking dog; and many will find the morals of the wolf prouder and more independent than those of the dog. We have only to refer to La Fontaine's fable.

True independent morals are those of the Good Samaritan, who tended the wounds of the Jew in spite of the religious hatred between Jerusalem and Samaria; they are those of Abd-el-Kadir risking his life to save the Christians of Damascus. Alas, venerable Pius IX, that you, Holy Father, were not able to risk yours to save those of Perugia, of Castelfidardo and of Mentana!

It was Jesus Christ who said, in speaking of the priests of His own times: 'Do what they say, but do not do as they do.' And then the priests said that Jesus Christ must be crucified – and crucifed He was! The priests, however shameful their works may have been, were infallible in their words.

On the other hand, did not the same Jesus Christ heal the sick on the Sabbath day, scandalizing the Pharisees and the doctors of the law?

True independent morals are those which are inspired by independent religion.

Now, this independent religion must be a manly one: the other sort is only good for children.

We could not have, in religion, a more perfect example than Jesus Christ. Jesus practised the Mosaic religion, but was not its slave. The law, He said, was made for man, not man for the law; He was rejected by the synagogues and spent little time in the temple; He took the side of the spirit against the letter on every question; unselfish love was all He enjoined on His disciples. His dying moments were spent in giving absolution to a penitent sinner and in commending His mother to the care of His beloved disciple, and the priests only assisted at His last hour in order to curse Him.

The point of balance in religion is the most absolute liberty of conscience and voluntary obedience to the authority which regulates public instruction, discipline and worship.

In politics, this point of balance is that despotism of the law which guarantees the liberty of all men within the most perfect hierarchic system.

In dynamics it is the central balance of a system.

In the Qabalah it is the marriage of the Elohim.

In magic it is the central point between resistance and action; it is the simultaneous employment of the *ob* and the *od* to create the *aour*.

In alchemy it is the indissoluble union of mercury and sulphur.

In all things it is the alliance of the true, the good, the beautiful and the just.

It is the proportionate measure of existence and life, it is eternity in time, and the power which generates time within eternity.

It is the part of the whole and the whole of the part.

It is the idealism of man meeting the realism of God.

It is the connection between the beginning and the end, and exhibits both the Omega of the Alpha and the Alpha of the Omega.

Finally, it is what the high initiates have designated by the mysterious name *Azoth*.

CHAPTER VIII
The End Points

The strength of magnets resides in their two extreme poles and their point of balance is in the centre between these two poles.

The action of one of the poles is balanced by that of an opposite pole, just as in the swing of a pendulum; the thrust on the left of the central point is proportional to the thrust on the right.

This law of physical equilibrium also applies to moral equilibrium: the forces are disposed at the extremities and converge on the central point. Between the ends and the middle the action is only weak.

The faint-hearted and indifferent are those who follow the current of public opinion, and are incapable of any movement by themselves.

The extremes are alike and meet by the law of the analogy of contraries.

They lend strength to any contest because they always preserve their separate identities while the contest lasts.

For example, after hot and cold have been mixed, they lose their characteristics of hot and cold and become lukewarm.

'What can I do for you?' Alexander asked Diogenes.

'Just step out of my sun,' answered the cynic.

Then the conqueror exclaimed: 'If I were not Alexander, I should wish to be Diogenes.' They were two arrogant individuals who understood one another and were able to make contact, although they stood at the two extremes of the social scale.

Why did Jesus seek out the Samaritan woman when there were so many respectable ladies in Judaea?

Why did He allow Mary Magdelene to wash His feet with her tears and caress them when she was a public sinner? Why was it? He has told you Himself: because she loved much. He did not conceal His preferences for people of ill repute like the tax gatherers and the prodigal sons. One feels, in reading His discourses, that a single tear brushed from the eye of Cain would be more precious in His sight than all the blood of Abel.

Saints have a habit of saying that they feel themselves to be no better than the vilest sinners, and they are right. Scoundrels and saints stand equal in the opposite pans of one and the same balance. Both parties rest on the end points, and it is just as far from a villain to a sage as it is from a sage to a villain.

These are life's exaggerations who keep life in balanced movement while ceaselessly joining battle. If the antagonism should cease while the forces are in manifestation, everything would come to a standstill in a fixed equilibrium, and this would be universal death. If all men were wise, there would be no more rich or poor, no servants, kings or subjects; and soon society itself would go out of existence. This world is a madhouse and in it the wise are the attendants; but a hospital is built above all for the sick. It is a preparatory school for eternal life; now the first requirement for a school is scholars. Wisdom is the end to be attained, the prize which has been offered. God gives it to those who deserve it, nobody brings it with them at birth. The equilibrant force is at the central point, but the motor force always appears at the extremities. Fools start revolutions, wise men finish them.

According to Danton, power belongs to the biggest villain in political revolutions. In religious revolutions, the fanatics will necessarily lead the others.

The reason is that great saints and great scoundrels are all endowed with magnetic personalities, because their wills have been inflamed by the practice of acts contrary to nature. Marat fascinated the Convention where everybody hated him, yet obeyed him as they reviled him. Mandrin dared to enter towns in broad daylight and hold them to ransom and no-one had the courage to try and arrest him. They thought he was a magician! They convinced themselves that if he were sent to the gallows he would act like Punch and hang the hangman: which is what he might well have done if he had not staked his whole prestige in an amorous adventure and had not allowed himself to be apprehended so ridiculously, like another Samson on the knees of Delilah.

Love for women is the triumph of nature. It is the glory of sages, but for brigands and saints it is the most perilous of all reefs.

The true love of bandits is the guillotine, which Lacenaire called his dear fiancée; and saints should only bestow kisses on death's-heads.

Blackguards and saints go to the same degree of excess and are equally the enemies of nature. We might add that popular legend often seems to confuse them with one another by attributing acts of monstrous cruelty to the saints and celebrating the kindhearted deeds of the outlaws.

Saint Simeon Stylites, perched on his column, was visited by his dying mother who wanted to give him a last embrace. Not only did this Christian fakir refuse to come down to her, but he hid his face from her. The poor woman died lamenting and calling her son by name, and the saint let her die. If anyone were to relate the same thing of Cartouche or Schinderhannes, we should think it a deliberate exaggeration of their wickedness; but then Cartouche and Schinderhannes were no saints, they were only common brigands.

O stupid, stupid, stupid humanity!

Derangements in the moral order produce derangements in the physical order, and these are what the average citizen calls miracles. One must needs be a Balaam before one can hear an ass speaking: the imagination of fools is the breeding ground of prodigies. When a man is the worse for drink, he thinks that everybody else is staggering and that nature herself is taking care to get out of his way.

Therefore you people who long to see something incredible, you people who want to perform wonders, make yourselves absurd in some way. Wisdom will never be noticed since it always resides in order, calmness, harmony and peace.

All vices have their immortals who have illustrated their shamefulness. Pride is Alexander, Diogenes or Erostratus; Wrath is Achilles; Envy is Cain or Thersites; Lust is Messalina; Gluttony is Vitellius; Sloth is Sardanapalus; Avarice is King Midas. Now set against these mock heroes, other heroes who arrived at exactly the same results by opposite means: Saint Francis, the Christian Diogenes who in his very humility posed as the equal of Jesus Christ; Saint Gregory VII, whose fits of anger threw

Europe into turmoil and compromised the papacy; Saint Bernard, the ghastly persecutor of Abelard, whose fame had eclipsed his own; Saint Anthony, whose filthy imagination surpassed the orgies of Tiberius or Trimalcion; the ascetics of the desert, always obsessed by the hungry dreams of Tantalus, and those poor monks who are always so greedy for gold.

As we have already said, the extremes meet, and whatever is lacking in wisdom has nothing to do with virtue. Folly is on its home ground at the extreme points; and in spite of all those dreams of mortifying the flesh and living in the odour of sanctity, folly, in short, always serves vice.

Evocations, whether voluntary or involuntary, are crimes. Those men who are tormented by the evil magnetic influence and to whom it appears in visible form, suffer the penalty of their outrages on nature. A hysterical nun is no less impure than a wanton: one lives in a grave, the other in a brothel; yet often enough the woman in the living grave entertains a brothel in her heart, and the woman in the brothel conceals in her breast a grave.

When the wretched Urbain Grandier, cruelly expiating the breaking of his rash vows, accused of being a would-be sorcerer and misjudged as a dissolute priest, went to his death with the resignation of a sage and the patience of a martyr, the pious Ursulines of Loudun, writhing about like bacchantes and gripping the crucifix between their legs, abandoned themselves to the most sacrilegious and obscene performances. People felt sorry for these 'innocent' victims! And Grandier, broken by torture and chained to his stake, being slowly burnt to death without a murmur of complaint, was regarded as their tormentor.

The unbelievable thing is that it was the nuns who represented the principle of evil, who brought it to fruition, who incarnated it in themselves; they were the ones who blasphemed, who cast slurs, who made accusations, and yet it was the object of their sacrilegious passion who was sent to his death! All Hell had been evoked by them and their exorcists, and Grandier, who had not so much power over them as to silence their tongues, was condemned as a wizard and a master of demons.

The celebrated curé of Ars, the scholarly Vianney, was, so his biographers tell us, plagued by a demon who lived with him on terms of familiarity. Hence the good curé was a sorcerer without knowing it; he was making involuntary evocations. How did this happen? We get the explanation from a remark he is alleged to have made. He is supposed to have said, in speaking of himself: 'I know someone who would be a big dupe if there were no eternal rewards!' Is that so?! Would he have stopped doing good if he had no hope of a reward? Was nature complaining at the bottom of his conscience? Did conscience feel it was doing an injustice to nature?

Surely the life of a wise man is recompense in itself? Does not he enter a happy eternity while still on earth? Is true wisdom ever the rôle of a dupe? Worthy man, if you did say this, it was because you sensed the exaggeration in your zeal. It was because your heart regretted the innocent pleasures you had lost. It was because mother nature scolded you as a thankless son. Blessed are those hearts which are not reproached by nature! Blessed are the eyes which look for beauty everywhere! Blessed are the hands which are always ready to bestow gifts and caresses! Blessed are the men who, given a choice of two wines, prefer the better, and are often more glad to offer it to others than to drink it themselves! Blessed are those affable faces with lips full of smiles and kisses! Such as these will never be duped, because the best thing in the world, after the anticipation of love, is the memory of having loved; and only those things whose memory is always a delight deserve to be immortal!

CHAPTER IX
Perpetual Motion

Perpetual motion is the eternal law of life.

Like human respiration, it manifests everywhere in attraction and repulsion.

Every action provokes a reaction; every reaction is proportional to the action which provoked it.

A harmonious action produces its harmonious counterpart. A discordant action necessitates a reaction which will look ill-regulated but will be, in reality, a balancing one.

If you fight violence with violence, you will perpetuate violence; but if you oppose it with the strength of meekness, you will enable meekness to triumph and violence will be broken.

Some truths seem to be opposed to one another, because perpetual motion causes them to triumph in turn again and again.

The day exists and the night exists too; they exist simultaneously but not in the same half of the globe.

There are shadows by day and twinkling lights at night, and the daytime shadows make the day sparkle while the glimmering at night seems to intensify its blackness.

Hence visible day and visible night are such to our eyes alone. The eternal light is invisible to mortal eyes and fills infinity.

Truth is the day of souls, and their night is falsehood.

All truth implies and necessitates a falsehood because forms are limited, and all falsehood implies and necessitates a truth in the rectification of the finite by the infinite.

All falsehood contains a certain truth which is the accuracy of its form, and for us all truth is enveloped in some falsehood where its semblance ends.

Thus is it true or even probable that there exists a tremendous individual or three individuals in one, who is invisible and rewards those who serve him by revealing himself to them, is present everywhere – even in hell – where he tortures the damned by hiding himself from them, desires the salvation of all and only bestows enabling grace on a very small number, and imposes a terrible law on all while allowing everything to cast doubt on its promulgation – is there such a God? No, no, and surely no, the existence of God as affirmed under this form is a truth in disguise and completely shrouded in misconceptions.

Must we accept that all things have been and all things will be, that eternal matter is self-sufficient, being determined in its form by perpetual motion, so that everything is force and matter, the soul is non-existent, thought is only a product of the brain and God is nothing more than the determinism of existence? No, indeed, for this absolute denial of intelligence would even contradict animal instinct. It is clear that the contrary affirmation necessitates belief in God.

Does this God reveal Himself outside nature in a personal way to men, on whom He imposes ideas which are contrary to nature and reason?

Of course not, because the fact of this revelation – if it existed – would be evident to everyone; and furthermore, even if the fact of an external revelation coming from an unknown being were an incontestable reality, if this being showed that he was in opposition to reason and nature which come from God, he could not be God. Moses, Mohammed, the Pope and the Dalai Lama each say that God has spoken to them to the exclusion of the others and has informed them that the others are liars. – So perhaps they are all liars?

– No, but they deceive themselves when they act divisively and say true when they agree.

– But has God spoken to them or has He not? God has no mouth or tongue to speak in the manner of men. If He speaks it is in our consciences and we can always hear His voice.

He it is who confirms in our hearts the words of Jesus, the wise words we find in Moses and the fine words we find in Mohammed. God is not far from every one of us, says Saint Paul, for in Him we live and move and have our being.

Blessed are the pure in heart, says Christ, for they shall see God. Now, to see God, who is invisible, is to feel Him in our conscience and to hear Him speaking in our heart.

The God of Hermes, of Pythagoras, of Orpheus, of Socrates, of

Moses and of Jesus Christ was one and the same God and spoke to them all. Cleanthes the Lycon was inspired like David, and the Krishna legend is as beautiful as the Gospel of Saint Matthew. There are admirable pages in the Koran; but there are stupid and hideous things in the theology of every cult.

The God of the Qabalah, of Moses and of Job, the God of Jesus Christ, of Origen and Synesius cannot be the God of the *autos-da-fé*.

The mysteries of Christianity as understood by Saint John the Evangelist and the learned fathers of the Church, are sublime; but the same mysteries when explained, or rather rendered inexplicable by people like Garassus, Escobar and Veuillot, are absurd and degraded. Catholic worship is splendid or despicable according to the priests or churches concerned.

Hence one may say with equal correctness that the dogma is true and is false, that God has spoken and that He has definitely not spoken, that the Church is infallible and that she is in a constant state of error, that she destroys slavery and conspires against liberty, that she elevates man and brutalizes him.

Admirable believers can be found among atheists so-called, and atheists among those who profess to be believers. What is the way out of these flagrant contradictions? It is to remember that the day has its shadows and the night its brilliant lights, and to pick out the good which is often found in evil and to avoid the evil which can mingle with the good.

Pope Pius IX published, under the name of the *Syllabus*, a series of propositions which he condemned, and most of them appear to be incontestably true from the point of view of science and reason. However, each of these propositions contains and conceals a false sense which is rightly condemned. Does this mean that we have to renounce what is, on the face of it, their true and natural meaning? When authority plays hide-and-seek, he who wants to do so may go looking for it; for our own part we shall not bother to recognize it until it shows itself.

The intelligent bishop of Orleans, the bellicose Right Revd. Dupanloup, has proved — by setting the Pope's own words against one another — that the *Syllabus* does not, and indeed cannot, mean what it seems to say. If it is a word-puzzle, we, who have not been initiated into the profundities of the court of Rome, must beg to be excused.

How many great truths lie hidden under dogmatic formulas which look very obscure or even completely ridiculous? Do my readers want examples? If one were to tell a Chinese philosopher that Europeans worship as the supreme God of the Universe a Jew who had been put to death by torture, one whom they resuscitate every day, so they think, in order to eat his flesh and bone under the outward appearance of a small wafer, would not the disciple of Confucius have some trouble in believing that nations which, in his eyes it is true, are barbarians but, when all is said and done, not total savages, could be capable of such enormities; and if one went on to say that this Jew was born to a woman who remained materially and physically virgin before and during her confinement, while a Spirit who is the same God as the Jew brooded over them in the form of a dove, would not his astonishment and scorn turn to disgust? But if, detaining him by his sleeve, one cried in his ear that the Jew who is God came into the world to die in torment to appease His Father, the God of the Jews (who found that He was not as good a Jew as they would like), and that the Jews' God abolished Judaism on account of His Son's death although He Himself had sworn it would be eternal, would he not become extremely angry?

Any dogma, if it is to be true, must hide beneath an enigmatic form a sense which is eminently reasonable. It must have two faces like the divine head of the Zohar: one of light and the other of darkness.

If the Christian doctrine as spiritually expounded, was not acceptable to a pious and educated Israelite, it would be necessary to say that this doctrine is false, and there is a simple reason for this: at the epoch when Christianity appeared in the world, Judaism was the true religion, and God Himself rejected, and had to reject everything which was not admitted by this religion. Therefore it is impossible for us to worship a man or any*thing* whatever. We must cling, above all else, to the theism and pure spirituality of Moses. Our interchange of language is not a confusion of the nature of things: we worship God in Jesus Christ, not Jesus Christ in the place of God.

We believe that God revealed Himself in humanity itself, that He is in us in the Spirit of the Saviour, who is the spirit of love, the spirit of piety, the spirit of intelligence, the spirit of knowledge and good counsel; and I see nothing which resembles a blind fantasy in all this. Our doctrines of the Incarnation, of the Trinity and of Redemption are as old as the world and spring even from that hidden doctrine which Mosaism reserved for its doctors of the law and its priests. The Tree of the Sephiroth is an admirable exposition of the mystery of the Trinity. The fall of Adam Kadmon, that gigantic conception of the whole of fallen humanity, demands a Restorer who is not less wonderful, the Messiah no less; and yet one who will reveal Himself with the meekness of a little child; able to play with the lions or call to His side the fledglings of the dove. Christianity, properly understood, is Judaism at its most perfect, minus circumcision and the rabbinic observances, and plus faith, hope and charity in marvellous communion.

Today's students take it for granted that the Egyptian sages did not worship dogs or cats or vegetables. The secret doctrine of the initiates was precisely the same as that of Moses or Orpheus. One universal God, as immutable as the law, as bountiful as life, revealed in the whole of nature, thinking in all intelligences, loving in all hearts, the cause and principle of being and of beings without merging with them, invisible, and beyond all thought, but certainly there because nothing could exist without Him.

Since they cannot see Him, men have dreamt of Him, and the diversity of gods is nothing more than the diversity of their dreams.

If your dream is not like my dream, say the priests of different cults, you will be eternally damned. Do not reason as they do; let us await the hour of reveille.

One could publish a fine book under a title already used by Michelet. It would be a harmony of the Bible, the Puranas, the Vedas, the books of Hermes, the Homeric Hymns, the maxims of Confucius, the Koran of Mohammed and even of the Scandinavian Eddas. This compilation, which would certainly be catholic, would be entitled to the name The Bible of Humanity; instead of doing this work, this rather too florid and stylish old man merely showed what could be done and lightly sketched the preface.

In essence, religion has never changed, but every age and every nation has its prejudices and errors. During the first centuries of Christianity people were anticipating the end of the world and disdained anything which might add comfort to life. In the face of dreams of Heaven, the sciences, the arts, patriotism, love of family, all fell into oblivion. Some ran to martyrdom, others to the desert, and the empire collapsed in ruins. Then along came the folly of theological disputes, and the Christians cut one another's throats over words which they did not understand. In the Middle Ages, the simplicity of the Gospels gave place to the quibbles of the schools, and superstitions swarmed everywhere. At the Renaissance, materialism reappeared, the great principle of unity was disregarded and Protestantism sowed freakish churches in the world. The Catholics were without pity and the Protestants were unrelenting.

Then along came gloomy Jansenism with its ghastly doctrines of the God who saves and damns by caprice; the cult of melancholy and death. After that the Revolution imposed liberty by terror, equality by the stroke of the axe and fraternity in bloodshed. There was a dastardly and perfidious reaction. Those interests which were threatened put on the mask of religion and the strongbox made common cause with the Cross. This is the situation as we find it today. The Zouaves have replaced the guardian angels of the sanctuary and the Kingdom of God, which suffers violence in Heaven, resists violence on earth, no longer with unworldliness and prayers, but with cash and bayonets. Jews and Protestants swell Peter's Pence. Religion is no longer a matter of faith, it is a partisan affair.

It is evident that Christianity has not yet been understood and that at last it is claiming its place; this is why everything breaks down and indeed will break down as long as it is not established in all its truth and in all its power to settle the world situation into a state of balance.

So the unrest we are experiencing is not being deliberately stirred up; it results from the perpetual motion which upsets everything which men try to oppose to its laws of eternal balance.

The laws which govern the world are also sovereign over each individual human destiny: man is intended to be restful without being idle. His restfulness consists in knowing his proper state of balance; at the same time he cannot renounce perpetual motion, because movement is life. One must either submit to it or direct it. To submit to it is to be broken by it, to direct it is to be regenerated by it. There must be an equilibrium between spirit and body, not an antagonism. The insatiable thirsts of the soul can be as baleful as the disordered appetites of the flesh. Lust is inflamed rather than assuaged by senseless privations. Bodily afflictions render the soul sad and impotent and she is not truly queen unless the organs, her subjects, are perfectly unconstrained and satisfied.

There is a balance and not an antagonism between grace and nature, for grace is the direction which God Himself has given to nature. It is by the grace of the Most High that the springs blossom, the summers come with fields of corn, and the autumns bear clusters of grapes. Why ever should we despise the flowers which charm our senses, the bread which sustains us, and the wine which invigorates us? Christ taught to pray to God to give us this day our daily bread. Let us also pray for the roses of each spring and the leafy shade of every summer. At the very least, let us ask Him for real affection in every heart, and an honest and sincere love for every creature.

There is a balance, in which antagonism must never interfere, between the man and the woman. Mutual devotion is the law of union which binds them. The woman must captivate the man by her charm, and the man must emancipate the woman by his intelligence.

If the woman is humiliated by the man, the man will be degraded by the woman. Buy a woman's favours and she will overcharge and ruin you. Turn her into a creature of flesh and filth and she will corrupt and defile you.

There is a balance, and not the slightest possibility of any real antagonism, between order and liberty, between obedience and human dignity.

Nobody has a right to arbitrary and despotic power. No, nobody, not even God. Nobody is the absolute master of anybody else. Even the shepherd is not the master of his dog to this extent. Protection is the law of the world of mind; those who must obey only obey for their own good; their will is guided but not subjugated; a person may enlist his will but never part with it.

To be king is to dedicate oneself to protecting one's royal rights against those of the people, and the more powerful the king is the more truly free the people are. For liberty without discipline and without protection is the worst of servitudes. It degenerates into anarchy, which is the tyranny of all in the conflict of factions. True social liberty is the absolutism of justice.

Human life alternates; Turn and turn about it wakes and then drowses, immersed by sleep in the collective and universal life; it dreams of its personal existence without any awareness of time and space. On its return to individual and responsible life, it dreams in the waking state of its collective and eternal existence. A dream is one of those glimmers in the night. A belief in religious mysteries is one of those shadows which appear in the depth of the day.

It is likely that, for man, eternity alternates like his life, being composed of periods of waking and sleeping. He dreams when he fancies himself to be living in the kingdom of the dead; he is awake when he resumes his immortality and remembers his dreams.

Genesis informs us that God cast Adam into a deep sleep and that while the man slept He drew from him the *Chavah* to give him a helper who was like him – and Adam exclaimed: 'This is now flesh of my flesh and bone of my bone.'

We are not forgetting that in the preceding chapter, the author of the sacred book has declared that Adam had been created male and female: clearly showing that Adam is not an isolated individual but is taken for humanity in its entirety. So what is this *Chevah* or Eve who comes out of him during his sleep to be his helper and who later will consecrate him to death? Surely, it is the same as the Maya of the Hindus, the corporeal receptacle, the terrestrial form which is the spirit's helper, similar to the spirit's own form but separated from it? When the spirit awakes from that earthly form, we call it death.

When the spirit sleeps after a day spent in the universal life, it gives rise to the *chavah* of itself; It wraps itself in its chrysalis and its periods of existence in time are only like dreams in which it rests from its labours in eternity.

Thus he ascends the ladder of the worlds, but only during his sleep. During his eternity he is able to enjoy all his fresh acquisitions of knowledge and power gained in union with Maya, whom he must use without becoming her slave. For Maya triumphant will throw around his soul a veil he cannot rend on waking, and once he has fondled that succubus he will be liable to wake up mad; and this is the veritable mystery of life eternal.

There are no more pitiable creatures than the mad, and yet, for the most part, they are unaware of their appalling misfortune. Swedenborg went so far as to say something which, dangerous though it may be, is not the less touching for that in our opinion. He said that the damned take the horrors of hell for beauties, its darkness for light and its torments for pleasures. They are like those condemned to death in some Eastern countries, who are stupefied with narcotics before being handed over to the torturers.

God cannot set aside the penalties attached to the violations of His law, but He considers that eternal death is bad enough without the addition of pain. Although unable to stop the furies as each draws her whip, He makes sure that those to be flogged are insensible.

We ourselves do not agree with Swedenborg's conception, because the only thing we believe in is everlasting life. His insane and hallucinated company of the damned, revelling in vile shadows and gathering poisonous toadstools in mistake for flowers, are punished for no useful reason as far as we can see, because they have no consciousness of their punishment. His hell, which would be a kind of lunatic asylum, is less noble than that of Dante: a circular abyss, continuously narrowing in its descent, and ending, behind the three heads of the symbolic serpent, in a strait way on which one need only turn round to climb back towards the light.

Eternal life is perpetual motion and, for us, eternity has no other meaning than the infinity of time.

Imagine for a moment that heavenly bliss consisted in saying Hallelujah, with palms in our hands and crowns on our heads, and that after five hundred million Hallelujahs we had always to start all over again (appalling bliss!), this would mean that a number could be assigned to each Hallelujah; it would have a predecessor and a successor, and succession entails duration, or time in other words — time, because there would be a beginning.

Eternity, however, has neither beginning nor end.

One thing is certain, and that is that we know absolutely nothing about the mysteries of the other life; but it is also certain that none of us recollects having started from nothing and that the idea of future non-existence imposes an equal strain on our intuition and our reason.

Jesus tells us that the just will go to Heaven, and calls Heaven His Father's House. He assures us that in this House are many Mansions. We would hazard a guess that these Mansions are the stars. So the idea, or theory if you will, of renewed existence in the stars may not be altogether out of keeping with the teaching of Jesus Christ. Dream life is essentially different from real life; it has its scenery, its friends and its memories; and in that life one possesses without doubt faculties belonging to other forms and other worlds.

One meets again loved beings whom one has never known on this earth; those who are dead are seen alive again; one is carried along in the 'air; one walks on water as if the action of body weight were less; one speaks unknown languages and makes contact with creatures who are very oddly organized. Everything there is reminiscent of so much that has nothing to do with this world; might these not be vague recollections of previous existences?

Do dreams spring from the brain alone? Well, if the brain produces them, who invents them? Often they terrify and tire us. What Callot or Goya invents our nightmares?

In our dreams, we frequently imagine we have committed crimes, and we are relieved to be free from blame when the hour of waking comes. Could the same thing be true of our veiled existence, our dreams beneath a covering of flesh? Did Nero wake up with a start and cry: 'Praise God! I have not had my mother assassinated.'?

Did he find her living and smiling beside him, ready to tell him in her turn, her imaginary crimes and evil dreams?

Our present life often seems like a monstrous dream, and is scarcely any more rational than the visions of sleep. One frequently finds in it things which cannot be, and the things which should be there are not. It looks to us sometimes as if nature is acting crazily and reason is arguing with itself under a frightful Ephiast. The things which happen in this life of illusions and vain hopes are doubtless as foolish in comparison with life eternal as the visions of a dream in comparison with the realities of waking life.

On waking, we do not blame ourselves for sins committed in our dreams, and, if they are crimes, society does not call us to account, if they have been committed while in a state of trance;

as when, for example, a man in a trance gives his wife a mortal blow while dreaming that he is killing her. In some such way as this, our earthly errors may have their repercussions in Heaven on account of a special exaltation by which man enters eternity before he has left the earth. Some of the acts done in our present life can disturb the regions of perennial serenity. There are sins which, in the common phrase, make the angels weep. Such are the unjust aspersions of the saints, the calumnies to which they expose the Supreme Being when they represent him as the capricious despot of spirits and the infinite tormentor of souls.

When Saint Dominic and Saint Pius V tortured dissident Christians, these martyred Christians having been readmitted by virtue of their shed blood into the great catholic assembly of Heaven, were no doubt welcomed into the ranks of the blessed spirits with cries of amazement and pity, and the terrible sleep-walkers of the inquisition would not have been excused when pleading, before the supreme Judge, that they had been raving in their sleep.

Perverting the human conscience, quenching the spirit and slandering reason, persecuting the wise and opposing the progress of knowledge, these are are the real mortal sins, sins against the Holy Spirit which can never be forgiven, neither in this world nor in the world to come.

CHAPTER X
The Magnetism of Evil

A single Spirit fills infinity. It is that of God, whom nothing limits or divides, who is everywhere entire and nowhere confined.

Created spirits can only live without sheaths which are suited to their environment, which are vehicles for their action while restricting it, and prevent them from being absorbed into the infinite.

If a drop of fresh water is thrown into the sea, it will lose itself there unless it is protected in an impermeable envelope.

Hence unclothed, formless spirits do not exist. The forms they have are relative to the environment in which they exist and, in our atmosphere, for instance, no other spirits can exist than men with the bodies in which we see them and those of animals whose destiny and nature is still unknown to us.

Do the stars have souls? Has the earth, on which we dwell, its own consciousness and intentions? These things are unknown to us, but we cannot prove that those who have chosen to believe them are wrong.

Certain exceptional phenomena have been explained as spontaneous manifestations of the soul of the earth; and as a sort of antagonism has often been observed in these manifestations, it has been inferred that the earth's soul is multiple. It has been said to reveal itself in four elemental forces which may be epitomized as two and are brought to a state of equilibrium by three. This is one of the solutions of the great Riddle of the Sphinx.

According to the ancient hierophants, matter is only the *substratum* of created spirits. God, they thought, did not create it directly, but certain powers, the Elohim, emanated from God and made the heavens and the earth. Their doctrine interpreted the first clause of Genesis like this:

Bereschith, the head or the first principle, *Bara* created, *Elohim*, the powers, *V'eth ha aretz* ... who are or who made (implied) the heaven and the earth.

We confess that to us this translation looks more logical than that which would give the nominative plural *Elohim* to the verb *Bara* used in the singular.

These Elohim or powers would be the superior souls of the worlds whose forms would be the substance which is specific to their elemental properties. In order to create a world, so it has been postulated, God linked together four guardian spirits who – while contending – produced chaos first, and then, having to repose after the struggle, composed the harmony of the elements. Thus the earth imprisoned the fire and swelled up to escape the inrush of water. The air escaped from the caves and enveloped the earth and the water, but the fire is always fighting and eroding the earth, the water invades the earth in its turn and rises to the sky in clouds; the air is provoked, and to drive away the clouds it forms currents and tempests. The great law of balance, which is the will of God, prevents the contests from destroying the worlds before the time appointed for their transfigurations.

Like the Elohim, the worlds are linked by magnetic chains which their revolt strives to break. Suns rival suns and the planets exert against planets, in opposing the chains of attraction, an equal energy of repulsion, in order to protect themselves from absorption and to preserve their individual existences.

These colossal forces have sometimes taken a shape and have appeared in the guise of giants: these are the egregors of the book of Enoch; terrible beings to whom we resemble the infusoria or microscopic insects which breed between our teeth and on our epidermis. The egregors crush us without pity because they are unaware of our existence; they are too big to see us and too limited to guess that we are there.

This explains the planetary convulsions which engulf whole populations. We know too well that God does not stop some stupid and cruel child from tearing the wings and legs from an innocent fly, and that Providence does not intervene in favour of the ant-hill which is destroyed and kicked to pieces by a passer-by.

Because a mite's organs defy human analysis, man thinks that he is entitled to suppose that his own existence is much more precious in the eternal scheme of nature than is that of the mite! Alas! Camoëns had probably more genius than the egregor Adamastor; but the giant Adamastor, crowned with clouds, girded with waves and cloaked in the hurricanes, would he have any conception of the poetry of Camoëns?

We look on the oyster as an appetizing morsel; we think it has no self-consciousness and therefore that it does not suffer. So, without the slightest remorse, we eat it alive. We toss the crayfish and the lobster into boiling water because, when cooked like this, their flesh is firmer and tastier.

By what terrible law are the weak abandoned to the strong and the small to the big, without the ogre having any inkling of the tortures he is inflicting on the poor wretch he devours?

Can we be sure then that anyone will come to our defence against beings who are stronger and greedier than we are? The stars act and react on one another; their equilibrium is produced by links of love and thrusts of hate. Sometimes the resistance of a star collapses and it is dragged into some sun which assimilates it; sometimes a star feels its force of attraction die within it and it is hurled from its orbit by the spin of the universe. Amorous stars approach each other and engender new stars. Infinite space is one vast city of stars; they consult together and communicate with telegrams of light. Some stars are sisters. Others are rivals. Necessity constrains the stars to follow their courses, but they can exercise their liberty in varying their emanations.

When the earth feels disagreeable, it fills men full of fury and unleashes plagues upon its surface; it projects a poisonous magnetism at the planets it does not like, and they retaliate by sending it war. Venus sheds upon it the venom of immorality; Jupiter provokes kings; Mercury sends the serpents of his caduceus against mankind; the Moon turns men into lunatics and Saturn drives them to despair. These fits of love and anger in the stars are the basis of all astrology, nowadays, perhaps, too much despised. Did not Bunsen's spectrum analysis recently prove that each star has its magnetism determined by a special and particular metallic base, and that there are scales of attraction in the sky like the gamut of colours? Thus there can exist, and indeed do exist, magnetic influences between the planetary globes; and these may obey the will of these planets, if they are endowed with intelligence or governed by those genii which were termed the celestial watchers, or egregors, by the ancients.

We observe astonishing contradictions when contemplating nature. Everywhere there are the evidences of an infinite intelligence, but we have also to recognize the action of completely blind forces. Plagues are but disorders which can be attributed to no principle of eternal order. Epidemics, floods and famines are not the decrees of God, and to attribute them to the Devil, that is to say to an angel of perdition permitted by God to work evil, is to conceive a hypocritical God who, in order to do evil, hides behind a responsible, depraved agent. So where do disorders really come from? From the errors of second causes. But if these second causes are capable of error, they must be intelligent and autonomous, and here we have the full doctrine of egregors.

According to this doctrine, the stars take no interest in the parasites which swarm over their epidermis but are wholly absorbed in their loves and hates. Our sun, whose spots signal its cooling, is being drawn slowly but inexorably towards the constellation Hercules. One day it will lack both light and heat, for the stars age and must die as we do. Then it will no longer have the strength to repel the planets, which will rush in and dash themselves to pieces on it, and that will be the end of our universe. But a new universe will arise from the wreckage of the old. A new creation will emerge from chaos, and we, reborn in a new species, will be able to fight to better advantage against the stupid grandeur of the egregors, and so it will go on until the Adam Kadmon has been restored. That spirit of spirits, that form of forms, that collective giant who sums up the whole of creation. That Adam who, according to the Qabalists, hides the sun behind his heel, conceals the stars in the tufts of his beard and, when he wants to walk, steps on the East with one foot and on the West with the other.

The egregors are the Anakim of the Bible or, rather, according to the book of Enoch, they are the patriarchs. They are the fabled Titans and are found in all religious traditions.

These are they who, in their battles, hurl meteorites through space, ride bareback on the comets, and fire salvoes of shooting stars and fire-balls. The air becomes unhealthy, the water corrupt, the earth quakes and volcanoes blaze with fury when these beings are angry or ill. At times, people coming home late in the valleys of the South of France are terrified to see the colossal form of a man, sitting quite still on the mountain plateau and bathing his feet in some lonely lake; they move on, crossing themselves at the same time, and think they have had a vision of Satan when they have only met the pensive shade of some solitary egregor.

These egregors, if their existence must be admitted, are the agents by whom God models, the living wheels in the creative machinery, as multiform as Proteus but always confined to their elemental substance. They would know the secrets of which immensity robs us but would be ignorant of some of the things we know. The evocations of the ancient magic are addressed to them and the barbarous names given to them by Persian or Chaldean are still preserved in the old grimoires.

The Arabs, who are the poetic guardians of the primitive traditions of the East, still believe in these gigantic genies. Some are black and some are white. The black genies are malevolent and are called Afreets. Mohammed has kept these genies; as well as angels so great that the beat of their wings sends the worlds sailing through space. We admit that we do not care for this infinite multitude of intermediary beings which hides God from us and seems to render Him useless. If the chain of spirits continually enlarges its links as it reaches back towards God, we see no reason why it should ever stop, for it will always go on into infinity without ever being able to touch Him. We should have millions of gods to overcome or to bow before without ever being able to arrive at liberty and peace. This is why we reject the mythology of the egregors finally and absolutely.

Here we draw a deep breath and wipe our brow, like a man who wakes up after an unpleasant dream. We look up at the heavens, full of stars but empty of phantoms, and with inexpressible relief in our heart repeat aloud the first words of the Nicene Creed: *Credo in unum Deum*. (I believe in one God.)

Hurtling down with the egregors and the afreets, Satan blazes out for an instant in the sky and disappears like a lightning flash. *Videbam Satanam sicut fulgura* (or *fulgar*) *de coelo cadentem*. (I saw Satan fall as lightning from Heaven).

The giants of the Bible were swallowed up by the flood. The mythological Titans were crushed beneath the mountains they

had piled up. Jupiter is only a planet and all the gigantic
phantasmagoria of the ancient world is nothing more than the
colossal peal of laughter named Gargantua in Rabelais.

God Himself no longer wishes us to represent Him in terms of
a monstrous pantheon. He is the Father of proportion and
harmony and rejects enormities. His favourite hieroglyphs are the
white and gentle figures of the lamb and the dove and He
presents Himself to us in the form of a baby in its mother's arms.
How adorable is Catholic symbolism, and how many
abominable priests have misconstrued it.

Can you imagine the dove of the Spirit of Love hovering in
the smoke of frying at the *autos-da-fé* and the Virgin Mother
watching the Jews burn? Do you see the wretched young men
who fall under the gunshot of the Zouaves of the Child Jesus and
the rifles ranged around the treasure acquired by indulgences?
But who can fathom the secrets of Providence! Perhaps this
misuse of military might will absolve the dissidents and the
pastor's sin will become the innocence of the world!

Besides, is not the Pope a saintly priest and does not he go
about his task with complete sincerity of heart? So, who is to
blame? – We must blame the spirit of contradiction and error,
the spirit of untruth which has been a murderer from the
beginning; we must blame the Tempter, the Devil, the
Magnetism of Evil.

The magnetism of evil is the fatal current of perverse habits, it
is the hybrid synthesis of all the voracious instincts and wiles
which man has copied from the most maleficent animals, and it is
really in this philosophical sense that the Middle Ages personified
demons.

The typical demon has goat's or a bull's horns, the eyes of an
owl, a nose like a vulture's beak, the claws of a Harpy and the
belly of a hippopotamus. What a figure for even a fallen angel,
and how far removed from the superb king of Hell dreamed up
by the genius of Milton!

However, Milton's Satan represents nothing more than the
revolutionary spirit of the English under Cromwell, and the true
Devil is always that of the cathedrals and the legends.

He is as crafty as a monkey, insinuating as a snake, as shrewd as
a fox, as ready to spring as a young cat, and as dastardly as the
wolf or the jackal.

He is as grovelling and as full of flattery as a valet, as ungrateful as a king, as vindictive as a bad priest and as conscienceless and perfidious as a wanton.

He is a Proteus who adopts all forms save those of the lamb and the dove, say the old grimoires. Now he is the knavish little page who carries the train of some grand lady; now he is an ermined theologian or a knight in armour. The evil counsellor slips in everywhere, he even conceals himself in the centre of the rose. At times, under the priest's cassock or bishop's cope, he trails his poor hidden tail down the church aisle; he clings to the nun's knotted cord and squeezes between the pages of the breviaries. He howls in the empty purse of the poor and through the keyholes of rich men's coffers he stealthily summons the thieves. His essential and ineffaceable character is one of perpetual absurdity, for morally he is a sot and is always engaged in some piece of stupidity or other. It is a waste of time to use trickery and to scheme and calculate; those who do wrong show their lack of sense.

According to the sorcerers, he invariably asks for something; he will accept a rag, a worn-out shoe or a piece of straw. No-one can fail to understand this allegory. If you concede the least thing to evil is it not the same as making a pact with it? If you summon it, even out of idle curiosity, are you not selling your soul to it? Legendary demonology is full of philosophy and reason. Pride, avarice and envy are not personages in themselves, but they are often personified in men, and those who end up by seeing the devil are looking at their own nastiness.

The Devil has never been good-looking; he is not a fallen angel, he has been damned from birth, and God will never pardon him since, as far as God is concerned he does not exist. He exists as our wrongdoing, he is vice, he is disease, he is fear, he is insanity and falsehood, he is the fever in the hospital of Limbo where sick souls languish.

He has never entered the serene celestial regions, and so could not have fallen from them.

Get thee behind me, therefore, thou impious dualism of the Manichees; get thee behind me, thou competitor of God, always powerful though struck down by the thunderbolt, and contending with Him for the world! Get thee behind me, thou valet who hast seduced thy master's children, who hast forced

God Himself to endure death to redeem the men who have been enslaved by the rebel angel, to whom, even so, He has abandoned the majority of those whom He wanted to win back by this inconceivable sacrifice! Down with this last, this most monstrous of the egregors! Glory and everlasting triumph to God alone!

Nevertheless, eternal honour to the sublime doctrine of the Redemption; our respects to all the traditions of the Universal Church; long live the ancient symbolism! But may God preserve us from materialistic interpretations and from taking metaphysical entities for real persons and allegories for histories!

Children love to believe in ogres and fairies and the masses need illusions; I know it, and agree with the nurses and priests on that matter. But I am writing a book of occult philosophy which is not intended for either children or the feeble-minded.

For some people the world would look empty if it were not inhabited by chimeras.

The depths of heavenly space would trouble them if they were not populated with little green men and demons. These big babies put me in mind of the man in La Fontaine's fable who thought he saw a mastodon on the moon while all the time he was looking at a mouse trapped between the lenses of his telescope. Each one of us has inside him his tempter or devil who is engendered by his temperament or temper. For some he is a strutting turkey-cock; for others he is an ape grinding his teeth. It is the brutish side of our humanity, it is the dark backdrop of our soul, it is the ferocity of our animal instincts exaggerated by the egotism of false and narrow-minded thinking, in a word it is the love of error found in spirits who despise the truth from cowardice or indifference.

The demon-possessed are so many that they make up what Jesus Christ called 'the world', which is why He said to His apostles: 'The world will kill you'. The Devil kills all who oppose him, and for anyone to consecrate his life to the triumph of truth and justice is to sacrifice his life. In the city of the wicked it is vice who reigns and the profit from vice which governs. The just is condemned in advance, there is no need for a trial; but eternal life belongs to the brave who know how to suffer and to die. Jesus, who went about doing good, knew that He was on the pathway to death and said to His friends: 'We are going to

Jerusalem, where the Son of Man must be handed over to execution. I am sacrificing my life; nobody is taking it from me; I am laying it down in order to take it again. If anyone wants to take me as his example let him shoulder his cross and follow me. You all see me now, but soon you will see me no longer.' 'Does He want to kill Himself?'; asked the Jews, on hearing Him speak like this. But to allow oneself to be killed by others is not the same as killing oneself. The heroes of Thermopylae were well aware that they were going to die there to the last man, and their glorious fight was certainly no suicide.

Self-sacrifice is never suicide; and Curtius, if he is more than a legend, was no suicide. Regulus, returning to Carthage, was surely not committing suicide? Did Socrates commit suicide when he refused to escape from prison after being sentenced to death? Cato, who disembowelled himself rather than submit to that megalomaniac, Caesar, is a shining example of a republican. The wounded soldier who, when fallen on the field of battle with no weapon left to him but his bayonet, plunged it into his heart saying 'Come and get it', when ordered to surrender arms, was not a suicide but a hero, faithful to his oath to conquer or die. De Beaurepair, blowing his brains out sooner than sign a shameful surrender, did not commit suicide; he sacrificed himself to honour!

If one makes no compacts with evil, one need not fear it; and when one does not fear evil, one ought not to be afraid of death, since it is evil which gives it its terrible empire. A black and frightful death, fraught with dread anguish, is the Devil's daughter. Both shall be destroyed; but, as they are liars, they profess to be eternal.

A little earlier, we said that the Devil is absurd and, in our *History of Magic*, we declared that he only makes us laugh; yet, to tell the truth, we do not laugh at an ugly absurdity and, when one loves that which is good, it is impossible to treat evil as a joke.

The astral fluidic vehicle, which is represented by a serpent in every mythology, is the natural tempter of the Chavah or of the material form; this serpent was as innocent as any other creature before Eve and Adam sinned. The Devil was born of the first disobedience and became the serpent's head destined to be crushed under the foot of the woman's seed.

The serpent as a symbol of the grand fluidic agent can be a sacred sign when it represents the magnetism of good, as did the serpent of brass of Moses. There are two serpents in Hermes' caduceus.

The magnetic fluid is subject to the will of spirits which can attract or project it with different degrees of force, depending on their state of exaltation or equilibrium.

It has been called the light bearer or *Lucifer*, because it is the distributor and specializer of the astral light.

It is also called the angel of darkness, because it is the messenger of obscure as well as of luminous thoughts, and the Hebrews, who called it Samaël, gave it a double character — white Samaël and black Samaël, the Samaël of Israel and the Samaël of the uncircumcized.

This allegory is obvious. To be sure, as Christians, we believe in the immortality of the soul; like all civilized people, we believe in punishments and rewards proportional to our works. We believe that spirits can be miserable and tormented in the next life; therefore we admit the possible existence of reprobates.

We believe that the chains of sympathy are not broken, but are, on the contrary, drawn tighter after death. However, this is only as far as the righteous are concerned. The only communication between the wicked is by emanations of hatred.

Therefore, the magnetism of evil may receive impressions from beyond the grave, but only through the perverse desires of the living; the dead who are punished by God have neither the power nor the effective will to do evil any more. Beneath the hand of God's justice one does not go on sinning, one pays the price.

What we deny is the existence of a powerful genie, a kind of black god, a dark monarch who is able to do evil after God has reproved him. To our mind, King Satan is an impious fiction, in spite of the poetry and grandeur with which it is expressed in Milton's epic. The guiltiest of the fallen spirits should have been cast down lower than the others and more securely chained by God's justice. It is true that prisons have their 'barons' who still exercise a certain influence over the criminal world, but this is a reflection on the inadequate means of surveillance or repression employed by human justice. Divine justice is not cheated.

In the apocryphal book of Enoch, we read that these black

egregors became incarnate to seduce earthly women and were the begetters of giants. The true agregors, that is to say the Watchers of the Night, in whom we prefer to believe, are the stars of heaven with their ever-twinkling eyes. They are the angels who control the stars and who are like shepherds for the souls which inhabit them. We also like to think that each race has its guardian angel or genie who could belong to one of the planets in our system. Thus, according to the poetical traditions of the Qabalah, Michael, the angel of the sun, is that of God's people. Gabriel, the angel of the moon, protects the children of the East who carry the crescent on their banner. Mars and Venus join in the rulership of France. Mercury is the genie of Holland and England. Saturn is the genie of Russia. All this is possible, if uncertain, and may be used in support of the hypotheses of astrology or of the fictions of the epic poem.

The reign of God is an admirable form of government, hierarchical in nature, where anarchy is self-destructive. If there are prisons in His empire for guilty spirits, God alone is their Master and makes sure that they are governed by angels who are strict yet good. It is not permitted to the inmates to torture one another. Can we say that God is less wise and good than men are? What, then, would we say of an earthly prince who chose a brigand of the worst sort to be governor of his prisons, and gave him leave to constantly sally forth to continue his depredations and set frightful examples to decent people and give them pernicious advice?

CHAPTER XI
Fatal Love

Animals are subjected by nature to a striking condition, called rutting, which urges them to reproduce their species. Only man is capable of a sublime sentiment which makes him choose his companion and tempers the carnal appetites by the most absolute devotion. This sentiment is called love. Among animals, the male mounts all the females indiscriminately and the females submit to all the males. Man is made to love an individual woman, and the woman who is worthy of respect keeps herself for her own man.

In men as in women, the allurement of the senses does not deserve the name of love: it resembles the rut in animals. Libertines, both male and female, are brute beasts.

Love gives an intuition of the absolute to the human soul, because it is absolute itself. It does not exist otherwise. When love reveals itself in a great soul, it is eternity which is revealed.

In the woman whom he loves, a man sees and adores divine motherhood, and bestows his heart for ever on the virgin whom he aspires to award with the dignity of mother.

The woman adores, in the man whom she loves, that divine fecundity which shall create in her the object of all her vows, the aim of her life, the crown of all her ambitions: the child!

So these two souls are only one which must be completed by a third. They are a single man in three souls as God is One in Three Persons.

Our intelligence is made for truth and our heart for love. This is why Saint Augustin spoke so truly when he said to God: 'Thou hast made us for Thyself, O Lord, and our heart can find no rest until it has found its rest in Thee.' Now, God who is infinite can only be loved by man by means of an intermediary. He causes Himself to be loved by the man in the woman and by the woman in the man. That is why the honour and happiness of those whom we love imparts to us divine grandeur and bliss.

When we love, we see the infinite in the finite. We find the Creator in the creature. When we are the objects of love, we are representatives of God; His ambassadors to a certain soul, fully empowered to grant it paradise on earth.

Souls live by truth and love; without love and truth, they suffer and pine away like the body when it is deprived of light and heat.

'What is truth?' Tiberius's representative asked scornfully when faced with Jesus Christ, and Tiberius himself posed a question with more insolent disdain and bitter irony: 'What is love?'

The rage at being unable to understand and believe anything, the frenzy at being incapable of love, this is the true definition of Hell; and how many men and how many women are delivered after this life to the tortures of this appalling damnation? How many are delivered to the passionate mania for falsehood; to the deceptions of love which consign the soul to fatal insanity? The need to know being always outstripped by the unknown and the need for love being always betrayed by the impotence of the heart?

Don Juan went on from crime to crime in the pursuit of love and was finally crushed to death in the embrace of a stone statue. Faust, when prompted by the emptiness of knowledge without faith, amused himself with the over-credulous Margaret, and was left with nothing but remorse after he had lost her. Perhaps Margaret will save him, because she, poor child, was really in love, and it is not God's will surely that she should be parted for ever from the one she adored.

Do you want to enter into the secrets of love? Study the mysteries of jealousy. Jealousy is inseparable from love, because love is an absolute preference which cries out to be reciprocated; but it cannot exist without that absolute trust which common jealousy naturally tends to destroy. The reason is that common jealousy is an egotistical sentiment, the usual result of which is to substitute hatred for affection. It is a secret calumny against the loved object, a doubt which insults it; often it is a frenzy which vents itself in ill-usage and destruction.

Therefore, judge love according to its works: if it elevates the soul, it will inspire devotion and heroic actions; if it is only jealous of the perfection and well-being of the one it loves, if it is capable of sacrificing itself to the honour and peace of the loved one, it is an immortal and sublime sentiment; but if it breaks the courage, enervates the will, lowers the aspirations, and perverts duty, then it is a fatal passion and one must conquer it or perish.

When love is pure, absolute, divine and sublime, it is in itself the most sacred of all obligations. We admire Romeo and Juliet in spite of all the prejudices and passions of the Capulets and Montagues, and do not think that Piramus and Thisbe should be separated for ever by their family feud. Yet we also admire Chimène asking for the death of Le Cid to avenge that of her father, because Chimène, by sacrificing love, made herself worthy of love; she felt sure that if she failed in her duty, Roderick would no longer esteem her. The heroine did not hesitate for a moment between the death of her lover and the devaluation of his love, and she justified that great saying of Solomon that love is more unyielding than Hell.

True love is a dazzling revelation of the immortality of the soul; for a man, its ideal is unstained purity and for a woman, unfailing generosity; it is jealous of the integrity of these ideals and one might term this noble jealousy 'Zelatype' or the standard of zeal. The eternal dream of love is the immaculate mother, and the dogma recently enunciated by the Church and borrowed from the Song of Solomon was revealed by love itself.

Impurity is promiscuity in one's desires. The man who lusts after all women, the woman who wants the desires of all men, do not know love and are not worthy to know it. Coquetry is the debasement of feminine vanity; even its name has an animal derivation and recalls the provocative strutting of the hens who want to attract the cock's attention. It is permissible for a woman to look beautiful, but she should only wish to gratify the one she loves or hopes to love one day.

The integrity of his wife's modesty is a man's especial ideal and is the subject of his legitimate jealousy. Refinement and magnaminity in her husband is the special dream of a woman and it is in this ideal that she finds the stimulus or failure of her love.

Marriage is legitimate love. A marriage of convenience is a marriage of despair. A male and female of the human species agree to propagate children under the protection of the law; if neither of them has yet come to love the other, one can but hope that love will develop in the intimacy of the family circle, but love is not always obedient to social conventions and those who marry without love often run the risk of adultery.

The woman who is in love and does not marry the man she loves is sinning against nature. Julie de Volmar is inexcusable and her husband is impossible, even in a novel; Saint-Preux must have been mistaken over this impossible pair. A girl who gets engaged and then jilts a man, dishonours her first love; it may be tacitly regarded as an earnest of adultery when she does marry. No woman worthy of the name need blush in the presence of the man who has shown himself worthy of her first love.

We can understand a tender-hearted man marrying, and rehabilitating in this way, a decent girl who has been seduced and abandoned; but that a girl should surrender herself when she is no longer her own mistress, and under the pretext that the baron d'Etange is threatening her life no less, or because she supposes that her father will die if she does not obey him, provokes us to comment that this indelicacy of heart is hardly justified by cowardice or a foolish sensibility. A father who talks of killing his daughter or of dying if she does not act becomingly and nobly, is no longer a father but a ferocious egotist, a despot one should reprove or fly from. In a word, Rousseau's Julie is a 'nice girl' who is not nice at all, but manages to betray two men at the same time. Her father is a pander who dishonours daughter and friend together; Volmar is a coward and Saint-Preux is an ass. Once he knew Julie was married, he had no business to see her again.

To marry a woman who is given to another and whom this other had not abandoned is the same thing as marrying someone else's wife. Such a marriage is null and void before nature and before human dignity. This is something which Rousseau did not understand. I will allow the happy-go-lucky marriages of Henri Murger's heroines, who treat life as a farce; but I will not admit the marriage of Julie, because she makes a show of taking love seriously. To be or not to be, that is the question, as Hamlet said; well, the essence of a human being is in his thoughts and in his affections.

For a person to abjure his thoughts publicly without being convinced of their falsehood, is an apostasy of the spirit; to forswear love when one feels its existence, is an apostasy of the heart.

Loves which change are passing whims; and those at which one must blush are misadventures whose influence ought to be shaken off.

Homer, in showing us Odysseus, after he had triumphed over the wiles of Calypso and Circe, ordering himself to be bound to the mast of his ship so that he could hear, without yielding to it, the seductive song of the sirens, gave us the true model of the wise man escaping the deceptions of fatal love; Odysseus owed everything to Penelope, who kept herself for him, and the nuptial bed of the king of Ithaca, with posts which were the eternal trees rooted deep in the earth, was, in the sometimes licentious days of antiquity, the symbolic monument to venerable and chaste love.

True love is an invincible passion motivated by right sentiment; it can never be in contradiction with duty, because it becomes in its own right the most absolute of duties; but unjustified passion constitutes fatal love and it is this which must be resisted even if one suffers and dies in doing so.

One could call fatal love the prince of demons, because it is evil magnetism armed with all its power; nothing can confine or disarm him when he goes on the rampage. It is a fever, a mania, a transport of delirium. The victim feels himself burn slowly and there is none to pity. Memories torture him, unfulfilled desires make him desperate; he entertains thoughts of death but more often prefers to love and suffer than to die. What is the cure for this disease? How can the wounds of this poisoned arrow be healed?

Who will rescue us from the aberrations of this folly?

To cure fatal love, one must break the magnetic chain by applying another current and neutralizing one kind of electricity with its opposite.

Put a distance between you and the one you love; keep nothing which reminds you of her; even get rid of the clothes she has seen you wearing. Take up tiring work of all sorts, never be idle, and never daydream; wear yourself out with toil during the day so that you will sleep soundly at night; find some ambition to fulfil, some interest to satisfy, and go higher than your love to find them. In this way you will achieve tranquillity, if not forgetfulness. What must be avoided at all costs is solitude, that nurse of the affections and dreams, unless one is drawn towards religious devotion, like Louise de la Vallière and like de Rancé, without intending to torture the body to relieve the agony of the soul.

Above all, it has to be understood that, as far as human sentiments are concerned, the absolute is an ideal which is never realized here below; all beauty alters and all life melts away; in short, everything passes with a marvellous rapidity; beautiful Helen has become a toothless skull, then a handful of dust, then nothing.

Any love which one cannot or should not declare is fatal love. There is no legitimacy in the passions outside the laws of nature and society. They must be exterminated at birth and suppressed with this axiom, *'That which must not exist does not exist'*. Nothing will ever excuse incest or adultery. These are shameful things, offensive to chaste ears even in name, and the pure must not allow their existence. Acts which are unjustified by reason are not human acts, they are bestial and foolish. They are falls from which one must recover, falls whose stains must be removed; they are acts of depravity which decency must hide, which morals, cleansed by the magnetic breeze, must not admit even to punish them. Look at Jesus, in the presence of the woman taken in adultery. He did not listen to those who accused her, he did not look at her so as not to see her blushes, and when they kept on pressing Him to judge her, He answered with these wonderful words which would be the end of all penalties imposed by human justice, if their meaning were not that certain acts must remain unrecognized and as it were impossible before the modesty of the law: 'Neither do I condemn thee, go and sin no more'.

This is how our sublime Master spoke to the unhappy woman whose accusers He had refused to hear.

Jesus does not use the word adultery; He calls it fornication, and for punishment He allows a man to send away his wife.

The wife, for her part, has the right to leave the husband who has deceived her. Then, if she has no children, she becomes free again before nature; but, if she is a mother, she loses her rights in her children by her husband, at least if he is not a notorious scoundrel. In renouncing him, she renounces her children; and if she has not the melancholy courage to leave them and lose their regard, she must resign herself to the heroism of maternal sacrifice, remaining a widow in marriage and consoling her misery as a woman in her maternal devotion.

Hen birds never desert their nests before the fledglings can fly, and why should women be inferior to the birds as mothers?

Love as an absolute ideal defies human generation in a certain respect, and this ideal demands the unity of love. The lovely dream of Christianity is the reality of noble souls, and it is because they would not sully themselves in the promiscuity of the ancient world that so many loving hearts entered the cloisters to live and die in an eternal desire. This occasionally sublime error is always regrettable. Ought one to refuse to live because one is not immortal? Ought one to stop eating because the food for the soul is better than that for the body? Ought one to give up walking for lack of wings?

Happy the noble Hidalgo, Don Quixote, who imagines he pays homage to Dulcinea when kissing the big, ill-shod feet of a peasant girl from Toboso!

Rousseau's Heloise, which we have just been criticizing so severely from the point of view of the absolute in love, is for all that a delightful creation, which is the more true for being defective, and reproduces in a truly human novel all the contradictions and weaknesses which made Rousseau a combination of the Don Quixote of virtue and a gossipy old retainer. After failing with Mrs de Warens, of whom he thought himself jealous, after losing his head over Mrs de Larnage, after adoring Mrs de Houdetot, who loved another, he philosophically married his housekeeper, and if it is true that the poor man died of a broken heart on discovering that Theresa had been unfaithful to him, one must admire and pity him, his heart was made for love.

There is only one woman in the world for the heart which is worthy of love, but the woman, this earthly divinity, sometimes reveals herself in several persons, and her incarnations are often more numerous than the avatars of Vishnu. Happy are those believers who never lose hope and, in the winter of the heart, await the return of the swallows.

The sun glows inside a drop of water. It is a diamond, a world. Blessed in the man who, when the drop of water evaporates, does not think that the sun has gone away. Passing beauties are only the fugitive reflections of the eternal Beauty, the unique object of our love affairs. I should like to have the eyes of the eagle and soar up towards the sun, but if the sun comes down to me, scattering his splendours in the dewdrops, I shall be grateful to nature without grieving too much when the diamond disappears. Alas! for that fickle creature who loves me no more in her search for her heart's ideal, I too was but a drop of water; must I accuse and curse her because, in her sight, I have become a fallen tear where she no longer sees the sun?

CHAPTER XII
Creative Omnipotence

That sublime passage at the beginning of Genesis is not the history of something which only happened once, it is a revelation of the laws of creation and the successive births of Being.

The six days of Moses are six lights which shine through the seventh. They are the genealogy of ideas which become forms in the order of eternal symbolic numbers.

On the first day, the unity of the prime substance was manifested. This is light and life and emerges from the shadows of the unknown.

On the second day were revealed the two forces which are the firmament, the firm placement of the heavenly bodies.

On the third day, the differentiation and union of the contrasting elements fecundated the earth.

On the fourth day, Moses bound up the quaternary traced in the sky by the four cardinal points with the circular movement of the earth and the stars.

On the fifth day, the power which could command the elements appeared, that is to say the living soul.

On the sixth day man was born with his animal helpers.

On the seventh day everything was in working order. Man was active and God appeared to rest.

The so-called days of Moses are the successive rays of light thrown by the Qabalistic numbers on the grand laws of nature, and the number of days are simply those of revelation. It is the Genesis of Science even more than that of the World, and it will repeat itself in every human spirit which searches and thinks. It begins with the affirmation of the invisible Being and, after the successive contributions of science, it ends in that repose of spirit which is faith.

Let us take a man who is in the vacuum of scepticism, or even systematically adopts Descartes' uncertainty.

'I think, therefore I am', he says with Descartes.

But do not go so quickly. Ask him, 'Do you feel that you exist?'

'I believe I exist' the sceptic will reply, and so his first word is a word of faith.

'I believe I exist, because it seems to me that I am thinking.' If you believe something and if it seems to be something to you, this is because you exist. So something exists, what we call 'being' exists; but everything is chaotic for you, nothing manifests itself harmoniously as yet and your spirit wavers in doubt as if it were floating on the waters.

It appears to you that you are thinking. Dare to say so clearly and boldly. You will dare if that is what you wish; thinking is the light of our souls; do not contend against the divine phenomenon which is going on in you; open your inner eyes; say 'Let there be light' and it will be for you. Thought is impossible in absolute doubt and if you admit thought you admit truth. Besides, you are really compelled to admit it, for you cannot deny 'being'. Truth is the affirmation of that which is and, in spite of yourself, you will find it necessary to distinguish it from the affirmation of that which is not, or the negation of that which is, the two formulas of error.

Keep silence now, and let us meditate in the darkness which gives us rest! You have just performed the intellectual creation proper to your first day! Now we must rise, for here is a new dawn! 'Being' exists and 'being' thinks. Truth exists, reality is an obvious fact, judgement is a necessity, reason assumes form and justice is indispensable.

Now go on to admit that 'being' has life. No proof is required for this. Obey your inner voice and take command of your sophistries; say, 'I will this to be' and it will be, for already quite independently of you it has to be and it is. Well, life is evidenced by movement, and the movement which occurs is conserved by equilibrium. Balanced movement is the separation between and relative equality of the alternate and opposite impulses of force. The first day has shown what substance is like, and the second day now reveals that force is dual. This double force, in its alternate and reciprocal impulses, constitutes the firmament or universal firmness of everything which moves according to the laws of universal equilibrium. You will see these two forces functioning in all nature. They push and they pull; they gather and they scatter. You feel them inside yourself, for you know the need to absorb and to radiate, to keep and to give. Blind instinct is balanced by intelligent foresight within you; you cannot deny the 'let there be', dare to affirm the 'is': say, 'Let equilibrium be in me' and equilibrium will be. This is your second day: the revelation of the binary.

Now distinguish between these powers, the better to unite them so that they will fertilize one another; irrigate the desert land of knowledge with the living water love; the earth is 'the science one works on and measures', faith is vast like the sea. Strengthen the dikes against its flood tides, but do not prevent it from raising the clouds overhead to shed rain on the earth. This will fecundate the earth; arid science will sprout and blossom. So much the worse for those who fear the waters of heaven and wish to hid the earth under a covering of brass. Let the eternal hopes germinate; let the simple beliefs flourish; let the great trees tower up. Symbols increase in magnitude like the cedars, they become deep-rooted like the oaks, and they have within themselves the seed which reproduces them. Love reveals itself in nature by harmony, the sacred triangle causes its light to shine, the number three completes the Divinity, either in your ideal or in your transcendent knowledge of yourself. Your intelligence has become a mother because it has been fertilized by the spirit of faith. Let us pause here, for this miracle of the light is sufficient glory for the third day.

Lift up your eyes now and gaze at the sky. Behold the splendour and ordered motion of the stars. Take a compass and an astronomical telescope and pile wonder on wonder. Calculate the return of the comets and the distance of the stars. All this proceeds according to the laws of a marvellous hierarchy. This whole immensity full of worlds absorbs and surpasses all the efforts of human intelligence. So is it intelligent? It is true that the suns do not wander where they will and the planets do not stray from their orbits. The sky is an immense machine which may not indeed think, but certainly reveals and reproduces thought. The four cardinal points of the heavens, the equinoxes and the solstices, the East and the West, the Zenith and the Nadir stand at their posts like sentinels and set us a riddle to guess: the letters of

the name Jehovah or the four elementary forms and the symbolics
of the ancient sphinx of Thebes. Before you learn to read, dare to
believe and avow that there is a hidden meaning in these writings
in the sky. If the orderly arrangement reveals a wise will to you
and if you still look on nature only as a machine which cannot do
anything on its own initiative, if you doubt that there is an
independent drive, shut your eyes and rest from the labours of
your fourth day. Tomorrow we shall show you the marvels of
autonomy.

The buzzing fly flits about and settles where it pleases, and the
worm crawls along in damp places to suit itself. These creatures
have something about them more surprising than the suns, for
they are autonomous and do not move like wheels in some
mechanism of fate. The fish is free and rejoices in the wave; it
rises to find its food on the surface; but a noise alarms it and it
escapes to the mud, lashing the water with its tail. The bird
cleaves the air as it goes its way; it chooses the tree or wall where
it will build its nest; then it perches and sings before looking for
twigs and grass; it promotes the birth of its little ones. Does it
think for itself or does something think for it? You are dubious
about the intelligence of the worlds, are you doubtful about that
of the birds? If the birds are free under an enslaved sky, whom
does the sky obey if not the One who has given liberty to the
birds? But the sky is no slave, it is subject to marvellous laws
which you can understand and the suns obey with no need to
understand them.

You have the intelligence of the heavens and on that score you
are greater than the heavens themselves. Are you the creator and
governor of the worlds? No, it goes without saying that this
Creator is someone other than you, but you are His confidant
and in a certain sense His coadjutor. Do not deny your Master,
that would be to deny yourself, child of Copernicus and Galileo.
You can create with them the heavens of science; child of the
unknown Creator, look at these myriads of universes which
inhabit space and bow before the sovereign intelligence of your
Father.

The star of intelligence, the mistress of the powers, the five-
pointed star, the pentagram of the Qabalists and the microcosm
of the Pythagoreans appears on the fifth day. You know by now
that matter cannot possibly move unless directed by spirit and

you require order in movement. You are going to understand man and you are going to make a synthesis to create him.

Here appear forms for all the forces of nature which are prompted by the supreme autonomy to become autonomous and living in their own right. All these forces will be subject to you and all shall conform to the likeness of your thought. Listen to the roar of the lion and you will hear the echo of your anger; the mastodon and the elephant make a mockery of your swollen pride; you resemble them, you, their master. No, you must tame them and make them serve your ends; but before you can impose your might upon them it is necessary to tame within yourself the vices some of them represent.

If you are greedy like the pig, lustful like the goat, ferocious like the wolf or thievish like the fox, you are only an animal disguised as a human being. King of the animals, assume your dignity and become a man; say 'I will be a man', and so you shall, because God wants you to be a man, but He awaits your consent for He has created you free. Why is this? It is because all monarchs must be acclaimed and proclaimed by their peers; it is because only liberty can understand and honour the divine power; it is because God needs this great dignity in man before man can legitimately adore God.

The occultism of God is as necessary as that of knowledge. If God were to reveal Himself to all men in a dazzling and irrefragable manner, the doctrine of everlasting Hell would be renewed in all its horror, and human crimes would no longer have any extenuating circumstances.

Men would be compelled to do good or be lost for ever, a thing which God could not possibly, and does not, wish. It is essential for doctrine to retain its integrity and for mercy to preserve its immense freedom.

God (if we may be permitted at this point, after the example of the great Qabalists and the inspired authors of the Bible to represent Him in human form), God I say has two hands: one He uses to chastise, the other to relieve and bless. The first is fettered by our ignorance and folly; the other always wishes to be free, and that is why God respects our own liberty and never compels our faith.

The human spirit is rapidly isolating itself from God. Forms of worship without authority are falling into a philosophy which is being swallowed up by materialism. The only secure religion, the one which can say *'non possumus'* ('we cannot'), has and always will have some potential, because it has the chain of instruction, the real efficiency of the sacraments, the magic of the creeds, the legitimate hierarchy and the miraculous power of the word. It is not perturbed by the rise of atheism and materialism, for those two hell-hounds have been unleashed to guard its portals and savage its enemies.

I know that a good many of my readers charge me with contradiction; they do not understand that I uphold the Catholic Church with one hand, and with the other strike out without pity at all the errors and all the abuses which have been, and still are, produced in its name and under its wing. Blind Catholics are shocked by my bold interpretations, and the self-styled freethinkers take umbrage at what they call my weakness for a religion which has fallen into disrepute because they have left it, or so they think. I am equally out of favour with the Christians of Veuillot and the philosophers who follow Proudhon. I am not surprised, I was expecting it, I do not distress myself over it, I do not even glory in it. I should much prefer to please everybody because I have a sincere love for all men, but when I have to choose between the truth and the esteem of anyone whoever, even one of my dearest friends, I shall always choose the truth.

Some say that the Roman Church is now no more than a shadow; a ghost staring into the past, which only knows how to move backwards; yet all the time they complain about her encroachments. She gets hold of the women and children, absorbs property, interferes with kings, clamps down on mass movements, and even presses into her service the gold of Jewish bankers and the blood of Voltaire's France.

This invalid, given up by so many doctors, makes a joke of Sganarelle's pills and refuses to die; for, in spite of the great thinkers and fine talkers, she holds the keys of eternal life. One feels that if she expired, God would steal away for ever from us, and the immortality of the soul would be gone.

There is a thing profoundly true which may perhaps appear paradoxical: it is that all the dissenting Christian sects only exist by the sublime stubbornness of radical Catholicism. Against whom would Luther and Calvin have protested, may I ask, if the Pope had yielded a little ground and given way to the Lutherans or

Calvinists? If the Pope were to concede, in principle, liberty of conscience, he would declare that, to him, his truth was doubtful. Now, to him, truth does not belong to a system, it does not belong to a sect, it does not belong to an imaginary religion, it belongs to believing humanity, it belongs to Hermes and Moses, to Jesus Christ, to Saint Paul, to Saint Augustin, to Fénelon and Bossuet, all of them greater thinkers and greater men than Proudhon, Dr Garnier, the sceptic Girardin and the nihilists Tartempion or John Bonhomme, do you understand? ... Do you understand?

No, the Pope must not say that in matters of religion we are free to think what we please. It is a strange way of interpreting liberty when the supreme head of an absolute Church is compelled to be tolerant when it is evident that tolerance would be the suicide of his spiritual authority. It is indulgence not tolerance that the representative of Jesus Christ owes to men and their errors. The Church is charity; everything which is uncharitable is contrary to her. Her only way of sustaining and perpetuating herself is by charity. That is to say, by the continual miracle of her good works which must prove her divinity to the world.

To assure her reign on earth, she must not enlist the zouaves, she must create saints. She must never forget this great saying of the master: 'Seek ye first the kingdom of God and His righteousness and all these things shall be added unto you.'

CHAPTER XIII
Fascination

The Church condemns magic and must condemn it, because she has made it her own monopoly. It is her place to use the occult forces employed by the ancient magi to deceive and subjugate the multitudes of their own day for the purpose, now, of the progressive enlightenment of men's spirits and for setting their souls free through the priesthood and morality.

This she must do on pain of death, but we have already said that she is immortal and that, for her, apparent death is potentially a work of regeneration and transfiguration.

Among the powers she commands, which can be used either for good or for ill, the power of fascination must be counted as one of the chief.

By fascination is meant the ability to make people believe the impossible, to see the invisible and to touch the impalpable; in other words, to take possession of the intellectual liberty of those whom one binds or looses at will.

Fascination is always the result of impressiveness.

When fascination is not achieved by falsehood, it is always brought about by some piece of impressive staging.

Take Moses when he was going to promulgate the Decalogue. He surrounded the most forbidding mountain in the desert with a barrier which might not be crossed on pain of death. At the sound of the trumpet, he ascended it to meet the Lord God face to face and, as evening fell, the whole mountain smoked amid a fearful display of thunder and lightning. The people trembled and fell on their faces; they could feel the earth shake; it seemed to them that the crags leapt like rams and the hills skipped like flocks of sheep. Then, as soon as the volcano had subsided, when the thunders had ceased, and the wonder-worker belatedly returned, he found the nation in a state of rebellion, determined to get hold of God for themselves at all costs. This was not what the Lord, Adonai, had intended. He was slighted and opposed by a golden calf. The flutes and tambourines parodied the trumpets and the thunder and the people, seeing that the mountains no longer danced, began to dance in their turn.

Moses, in a rage, broke the tables of the law and turned the performance into a great massacre. The feast was drowned in blood and the vile multitude, seeing the flashing blades remembered the lightning flashes and began to believe once more; they could no longer look Moses in the face; the most terrible of law-givers shone with the light of Adonai, he had horns like Bacchus and Jupiter Ammon, and henceforward he no longer showed himself with a veil over his face, so that his dread might be lasting and the fascination might continue. No-one, from then on, could resist with impunity this man whose wrath could strike like the sand-storm and who had the secret of the thunders and the inextinguishable flames. There is no doubt that the Egyptian priests had a knowledge of science well in advance of ours, and as we have already said, the Assyrian Magi were acquainted with electricity and could imitate thunder.

With that difference which there is between Jupiter and Thersites, Moses held the same opinions as Marat. He believed, that for the health of a people who were destined to be a light to the world, a Pontiff of the future should not recoil from bloodshed. What prevented Marat from being the Moses of France? Two important things: genius and success. Besides, Murat was a grotesque pygmy and Moses was a giant, if we can believe the divine intuition of Michelangelo.

Dare we say that the Hebrew legislator was an impostor? One is never an impostor when one is dedicated. This master who dared to play on the terrible instrument of death with such an air of omnipotence was the first to anathematize himself in expiation of the blood shed; he led his people to a land of promise which he knew that only he would not enter. He disappeared one day among caverns and precipices like Oedipus in the tempest and those who admired his genius were unable to recover his bones.

The wise men of the ancient world, being convinced of the necessity of occultism, carefully concealed those sciences which to a certain extent made them masters of nature, using them to give their teaching the prestige of divine co-operation. Why blame them? Is not the sage God's plenipotentiary among men? And when God allows His thunderbolt to slumber or awake, is it not always He who thunders by the agency of His ambassador?

One would have to certify the man who was mad enough to say, 'I have scientific proof that God exists', but the man who dared to say, 'I know that God does not exist; I believe in God but I don't know what I believe in,' would be even more of an idiot. Yet thousands of men, women and children will tell you, 'I have seen Him, I have touched Him, and I have gone further than that – I have eaten Him and have felt Him living within me.' Such is the strange fascination of an irrational saying (if that is really what it is): 'This is my flesh, this is my blood', which is nevertheless victoriously convincing because it is so delightful to set reason aside and gratify the feelings.

He uttered this saying, yes He, the God who was going to die so that He could live again in all men. Men of faith, you alone understand how God Himself must die so that we can accept the mystery of death!

God became son of man so that men could become sons of God. God incarnate imparted divinity to humanity. If you wish to see God, look at your brothers. If you mean to love God, love one another. This sublime and triumphant faith is going to inaugurate the reign of universal fellowship, of the most exalted love, of devotion to the poor! Whatever you do for the least, that is to say for the most ignorant, the most blameworthy of your brothers, you do for Me, for God. Can you comprehend this, you miserable inquisitors? Don't you see you have tortured Jesus Christ, you have consigned God to the flames ...!?

Certainly, poetry is greater than science; and faith is imposing and magnificent when it overrides reason. The sacrifice of the just for the unjust in unreasonable, but even the most egotistical reason is compelled to admire it. Here is the great fascination of the Gospel, and I confess that, at the risk of being taken for something of a fool, I the enemy of dreams, I the opponent of any imaginations which would impose themselves on knowledge, yes even I remain fascinated and am glad to be; I worship with my eyes closed against hostile sparks of light, because I cannot help believing in a boundless though still veiled illumination promised by that infinite love which I feel shining in my heart.

All great sentiments are forms of fascination and all truly great men have swayed the masses with their fascination. '*Magister dixit*' – 'The Master has spoken.' This is what motivates those who are born into eternal discipleship. '*Amicus Plato sed magis amica veritas.*' – 'I love Plato but I prefer the truth,' is the word of a man who senses that he is Plato's equal and consequently is potentially a master himself if he possesses, like Plato or like Aristotle, the ability to fascinate and inspire a school.

Jesus, in speaking of the people who follow the crowd, said, 'I will that when they look they shall not see, and when they listen they shall not understand, because I apprehend danger from their conversion and I fear their healing.' On reading these terrible words by the One who sacrificed Himself in philanthropy, I am reminded of that Crispinus of whom Juvenal said, '*At vittiis aeger solaque libidine fortis*' – 'Exhausted by every vice, his only remaining energy is the fever of debauchery.' What compassionate physician would have wished to cure Crispinus' fever? That would have signed his death warrant.

Woe to the ungodly masses who are no longer fascinated by the ideal of the superior powers! Woe to the poor fool who, fool that he is, no longer believes in the divine mission of the priests or in the divine right of kings! For he needs must be fascinated by something, whether by gold or by brute pleasures, and will find himself fatally excluded from the company of truth and justice.

Nature herself, when she intends to compel living creatures to perform her great mysteries, assumes the character of a sovereign priestess, fascinating at one and the same time their senses, their spirits and their hearts. There are two fatal magnetic forces which, when they meet, form an invincible providence called love. The woman is transformed into a sylph, a peri, a fairy, an angel. The man becomes a hero, almost a god. When they are sufficiently deceived, these poor innocents who adore one another's spurious appearance, they prepare themselves for the hour of satiety and sad awakening! The great secret of marriage is to defer this hour. At all costs one must prolong the error, feed the folly and perpetuate the unguessed deception. Life is then a play in which the husband must be a superlative actor, always on stage if he does not wish to be tricked like Pantaloon in the Italian farce; a comedy in which the wife must study her role of coquette to perfection, always concealing her more legitimate desires if she hopes to retain her husband's desire. Domestic bliss is won at the expense of a hidden battle – tiring and difficult, but unfortunately essential if open conflict is to be avoided.

Humanity has two great powers: the genius which fascinates and the enthusiasm which comes of fascination. Do you see this pale little man marching at the head of an immense army of soldiers? Ask where he is taking them. An onlooker with no illusions would say 'To death!'; they themselves, with moustaches bristling and shouldered arms, would cry 'To glory!' All these veterans are believers of Polyeuctus' stamp; they submit to the fascination of a grey frock-coat and a little hat. Kings salute them and take off their crowns as they pass and, when they are being crushed at Waterloo, these men grumble at the showers of grape-shot as they would at the weather and fall where they stand, defying death with a coarse oath from the mouth of Cambronne.

Animal magnetism does exist, but beyond that, which is purely a physical thing, we have to reckon with human magnetism which is the true moral magnetism. Souls are polarized just as bodies are, and spiritual or human magnetism is what we call the power of fascination.

The radiation of a great thought or of a powerful piece of imagination in man sets up an attractive vortex which soon draws planets to the intellectual sun, and satellites to the planets. A great man in the starry regions of thought is like a hub of the universe.

Imperfect beings who are not fortunate enough to be captivated by an intelligent fascination, fall into bondage to fatal fascinations. This is how giddy passions and delusions of grandeur are produced in imbeciles and fools.

There are enlightening fascinations and there are dark fascinations. The Thugs of India were enamoured of death. Marat and Lacenaire had blind supporters. We have already said that the Devil is the caricature of God.

Coming now to the definition of fascination: it is the magnetism of imagination and thought. It is the domination exercised by a strong will over a weak one to heighten imaginary concepts and to influence the judgement of beings whose reason has not yet reached a state of equilibrium.

The well-balanced man is the one who can say, 'I know what is, I believe in what must be and I do not deny what can be.' The subject of fascination will say, 'I believe what I have been told to believe by the persons I trust; in other words, I believe because it suits me to believe. I believe because I love certain persons and certain things.' Here we may find him using various touching phrases which prove nothing, such as 'The faith of our Fathers', 'My Mother's Cross.' In other words, the first says 'My beliefs stem from reason', while the second says 'My beliefs are governed by fascination.'

To believe on the word of others is something which is permissible and even advisable for children. If you reply that Bossuet, Pascal and Fénelon were great men and yet they believed in manifest absurdities, I shall answer that I find it hard to take this view but that even if it were true it would only prove that these great men behaved like children in some instances.

Pascal, we are told, constantly saw a pit yawning in front of him. It seems to me, without any disrespect to Pascal's genius, that there is no need to believe in his pit; the man who is fascinated loses his free will altogether and falls completely under the domination of the fascinator. Although his reason functions perfectly for neutral subjects, it changes absolutely into a state of folly as soon as you try to correct the things which have been suggested to him. He only sees and hears through the eyes and ears of those who are dominating him. Let him touch the truth and he will maintain that what he touches does not exist. On the contrary, he believes that he sees and touches the impossibility which has been affirmed to him. Saint Ignatius composed certain spiritual exercises for cultivating this kind of fascination in his disciples. He laid it down that every day the Jesuit novice should retire to a dark and silent place and employ his imagination in creating a perceptible representation of the mysteries, that he should try to see, and indeed see as real, all the nightmares of Saint Anthony and all the horrors of Hell in a voluntary and waking dream imposed on a wearied brain. During such exercises the heart hardens and atrophies from terror, the reason totters and dies. Ignatius has destroyed the man but has made a Jesuit, and the whole world will not be as strong as this formidable android.

Nothing is as implacable as a robot. Once it has been set going it will not stop until you have smashed it.

What Loyola did was to create thousands of robots which

could be started at a word and sent marching across the world to carry out by all possible means the intentions of the engineer. It must be admitted that his invention is far greater than Pascal's computing machine.

But is such a work moral? Yes, of course, in the thought of its author and of all those who are so devoted that they think they are doing the right thing to become blind cogs like this and automatons without autonomy. Evil will never work men up to this point, nor will reason or even ordinary common sense inflame them in such a way. Philosophy will never have such soldiers. Democracy may have its partisans and martyrs, but never its veritable apostles capable of sacrificing their self-respect and their entire personality on its behalf. I have known and I still do know worthy democrats, and each of them represents the strength of one isolated individual. The name of the Jesuit is Legion. Why are men so cool when reason is involved and so warm when it comes to fighting for some figment of their imagination? It is because man, in spite of all his pride, is defective; he does not have a sincere love of the truth, but on the contrary worships illusions and lies.

'Seeing that men are foolish,' said Saint Paul, 'we have endeavoured to save them even by foolishness, imposing what is good on the blindness of their faith.' Here the great secret of Saint Paul's Catholicism grafted on the Christianity of Jesus awaits completion by the Jesuitism of Saint Loyola. The masses thrive on absurdities. Society is made up of a small number of wise men and a great herd of stupid people. Now the government of the stupid by the wise is what is desirable.

How can this be managed? As soon as the wise man shows that he is wise, he is repulsed, slandered, exiled and crucified. People do not want to be convinced, they want someone to impose on them. Hence the apostle must seem to be dealing in imposture in order to revive, that is to say to regenerate truth in the world by giving it a new veil. How can we define a revealer? He is a disinterested imposter who, in order to turn them in the direction of good, is prepared to deceive the common masses. So who are these common masses? They are the immense crowd of dolts, imbeciles and fools whatever their titles, their place in society and their wealth.

I am aware that there is much talk of indefinite progress, but I should prefer to call it indefinable progress, for if the human race is increasing in knowledge it is not improving in itself. Another saying is that to enforce universal education would be to eradicate crime, as if education would necessarily make men better, as if Robespierre and Marat, the frightful disciples of Rousseau, had not received a superior education to Rousseau's own. The abbé Coeur and Lacenaire were pupils at the same college. Mr de Praslin, and Dr Castaney and Dr Lapommeraye enjoyed all the benefits of a modern education. Eliçabide studied at the seminary. Educated scoundrels are the most well-equipped and the most dreadful of all scoundrels and teaching has never stopped them from doing wrong, whereas simple illiterates find no difficulty in practising the finest virtues. Education develops a man's faculties and gives him the means of following his inclinations, but it does not change him. If you teach mathematics and astronomy to a dolt you might transform him into a Leverrier but you will never make a Galileo of him.

The human race as we know it is composed of one or two men and a large number of composite creatures with a little of the man in them and a great deal of the orang-utan or gorilla. Maybe some can claim a resemblance to the smaller and prettier apes: these are the gigolos who are the slaves and playthings of some loose woman. I wonder whether there is any paradise prepared for these animals, or any hell for that matter.

When these brute beasts are at the point of death, their human side, such as it is, sometimes awakens and torments them; they call for a priest, the priest comes and why not?

Charity would not extinguish these glimmers of humanity, but what can one say to them? They will understand no appeals to reason, so they must be fascinated by signs, by unctions, by benedictions and by absolutions *in extremis*. They are shown an embroidered stole and a silver-gilt ciborium. They say what they are told to say, allow everything to be done to them which may be required and die peacefully with the blessing of the Church. Is it not written in the Gospel that God will save both men and animals – *Homines et jumenta salvabis, Domine*.

Nature's creations are successively progressive as to species and races, but both races and species rise and fall like empires and individuals. All nations which have had their shining eras gradually fade away, and as it is with nations so it will be with

humanity as a whole. When men who are half beasts disappear in
the next cataclysm, we do not doubt that a new race of wise and
powerful beings will appear who will bear the same proportion
to our species as we bear to the monkeys.

It is only then that souls will be truly immortal, for they will
become worthy and capable of retaining their memory.

Meanwhile it is certain that, far from evolving, the human race
is actually degenerating. A fearful phenomenon is occurring in
our souls. Men no longer have any feeling for the divine and
those women who are not machines of vanity and luxury only
turn to faith out of liking for the absurd, as a refuge from reason,
which bores them. Poetry is dead in our hearts. Our young
people read Victor Hugo, but all they admire in this poet is the
fine writing and his quotable thoughts; deep down they prefer
Proudhon, find too much sensibility in Renan and treat Mr Taine
and Dr Grenier and Dr Buchner as serious writers. The theatre
goes out of its way to poke fun at all the generous sentiments of
former times; not with the loud peal of laughter of Rabelais
when he was castigating human stupidity, but with the sneer of a
broad joke which offers an insult to all the virtues.

As with honour so with love, it is an old saint who has no
more praise. Even the names of the grandest and most beautiful
sentiments are almost out of place in polite conversation and it
may soon be considered improper to repeat them. What are the
dreams of the really nice young ladies who lead the most
sheltered lives, those for example who attend the Oiseaux or
Sacré-Coeur convent schools? Are they longing for the
tenderness of mutual affection? Not a bit of it, that would be a
matter fit for the confessional and none of them would dare
admit such a thing to her friends. They think about the
splendours of a rich marriage and dream of a carriage and a
castle. If they can get a husband with a distinguished name and
good appearance, they will not mind having to take him as part
of the deal.

I am not a misanthropist and I am not trying to satirize my
century, I am recording a moral weakness in the human species in
order to show that Magism is more than ever timely and that
when one is dealing with such poor material it is necessary to
fascinate if one is going to succeed.

There are precepts in the Gospels the sublimity of which was felt in other days; but in our days they seem almost ridiculous because people are no longer what they were.

'Go and sit in the last place,' says Jesus, 'and you will be invited to take the first.'

To which the modern world replies, 'If you sit down in the last place you will have to stay there and it will serve you right.'

'If some one wants to take away your coat, let him have your cloak also' says the Gospel.

'And when you are completely naked the highwayman will give you his blessing and the police will arrest you for indecent exposure', comments the dry logician.

'Take no thought for the morrow,' says the Saviour.

'And on the morrow when misery overtakes you, no-one will think of you,' is the world's retort.

'Seek ye the Kingdom of God and His righteousness and all these things shall be added unto you.'

'Yes, once you have found, but not while you are looking, and I fear you may have to look for a long time.'

'Woe to those who laugh for they shall weep; blessed are they who weep for they shall laugh.'

'With respect, this is like a see-saw; it is the same as saying: "blessed are the sick for they shall get well and woe to those who are well for they shall become sick." If those who laugh are wretched and if you have nothing to promise to the happy people who weep than the misery of laughing in their turn, who then will be truly happy?'

'Do not resist the wicked person: if someone strikes you on one cheek, turn the other.'

'This is a positively immoral maxim. If you do not resist the evildoer you are his accomplice. If you turn the other cheek to somebody who has struck you unjustly, you are approving his offence and provoking him to repeat it; after you have offered your other cheek and received a second buffet, what will you do then? Fight him? This would make your recent behaviour pointless. Turn your back so that he can kick your posterior? That would be ignoble and ludicrous!'

This is how the spirit of our age would respond to what are probably the most sublime sayings in the Gospels, if it had the courage of its convictions to speak so freely. There is and must be a huge misunderstanding between Jesus Christ and mankind.

Our era has no longer any feeling for the sublime or any understanding of heroes. Our politicians see Garibaldi as a not very funny incarnation of Don Quixote.

He is a sober clown who, after beating a few commissaries and after the crafty have played cat and mouse with him, will end up one day by being carried off by the Devil to the great amusement of the spectators.

'The world is without religion', said Count Joseph de Maistre, and it is for this reason, let us add, that it stands in need of marvels and jugglers.

When folk no longer believe in the priest they will believe in the sorcerer and we have written our books chiefly for priests so that, having become genuine magicians, they need no longer fear the illegal rivalry of the sorcerer. The author of this book belongs to the great sacerdotal family and has never forgotten it.

Let the priests become men of science once more and astonish the degenerate world by their grandeur of character; let them put behind them petty interests and passions; let them perform miracles of philanthropy and they will have the world at their feet; let them lay their hands on the sick and heal them as the zouave Jacob has done; in a word let them learn how to fascinate and they will learn how to reign.

Fascination has a big role to play in medicine, a doctor's big reputation heals his patients in advance. A blunder by Mr Nélaton (if the celebrated practitioner were capable of such a thing) might do more good than all the skill of an ordinary surgeon. The story is told of a famous physician who, on handing his prescription for a plaster to the nurse looking after a man in great pain, said, 'Apply *this* to his chest at once'. The good woman, who was not very bright, thought he was talking about the prescription itself and slapped it hot with a little linseed oil on her patient. The latter felt relieved straight away and by the next day he was cured.

This is how big doctors heal our bodies and how accredited priests are able to cure our souls.

When I speak in this chapter of the beginning of a human decline, I am only talking of the phenomena which have come under my observation and I am not concluding that the entire species is in a state of decay on the evidence of the enfeeblement of a race. In spite of so many sad symptoms, I hope that there may still be progress before the destruction, or rather before the transformation, of man. I believe we have yet to see the realization of the Messianic hope which will regenerate a long succession of centuries. I trust that the last word on the human species will not be that on the civilizations of Nineveh, Tyre, Babylon, Athens, Rome and Paris. I like to think that what could be taken for decrepitude is nothing more than the easy tiring of childhood. Yet even Messianism is not the doctrine of eternity; there will be, says Saint John, a new heaven and a new earth. The New Jerusalem will only come through new nations superior to present-day man, and there will be even further changes. When our sun is an opaque planet of which we are the satellite, who knows where we shall be then or under what form we shall be living? One thing is certain: being is being. It does not come out of some nothingness which, being nothing, can give rise to nothing; and it will not return to that nothingness from which it could not have come.

All that is has been, is and will be.

Ehied ascher Ehieh. אהיה אשר אהיה ('I am that I am.' Exod. 3:14)

To revert to fascination and the means of producing it, these means are entirely in the power of the will energizing itself without strain and perservering calmly.

If you do not behave extravagantly but come to a reasonable belief that you are someone big and strong, the weaklings and nonentities will necessarily take you for what you believe yourself to be. It is all a question of patience and time.

We have already said that there is a purely physical attraction which is a part of magnetism. Some individuals are naturally endowed with it and one can induce it in oneself by gradually exciting the nervous system.

The celebrated Mr Home who now and then exploited in a rather charlatan fashion this unusual faculty, possessed it without being able to account for it, his intelligence being too limited for scientific studies. The zouave, Jacob, is a naïve fascinator who believes in spirit helpers. The agile conjurer Houdin mixes fascination and dexterity. A distinguished nobleman of our acquaintance asked him one day for lessons in white magic, and

Robert Houdin taught him certain things but remained silent about others which he declared he was unable to teach. 'I myself cannot account for these things,' he said 'they are a part of personal nature. If I told you them you would hardly be any the wiser and I could never put you in a position to make use of them'.

It is, if you will pardon the expression, the art or faculty of throwing dust in people's eyes. So you see, all types of magic have their ineffable arcana, even the white magic of Robert Houdin.

We have said already that it is a highly philanthropic act to fascinate simpletons to make them accept truth as if it were a lie and justice as if it were partiality and privilege, shifting the object of their egotism and covetousness so that they will be self-sacrificing down here in the hope of an immense and exclusive inheritance in Heaven.

But we must also say that all those who consider themselves worthy to be called men must, at the same time as they go along with the error of the young and weak, exert their reason and intelligence to the utmost to avoid being fascinated themselves.

Disillusionment is a cruel experience when there is nothing to replace the illusion, and vanished mirages and extinguished will-o'-the-wisps leave the soul in darkness.

It is better to believe in absurdities than to believe in nothing; there is more value in being a dupe than in being a corpse. Nevertheless, wisdom precisely consists in a knowledge which is sufficiently solid and a faith which is sufficiently reasonable to exclude doubt. Doubt is really a groping ignorance. The wise man knows certain things and what he knows leads him to postulate the existence of what he does not know. Such a postulate is faith, which is no less certain than knowledge when it confines itself to necessary hypotheses and is not rash enough to define the indefinable.

A man who is really a man understands marvels without submitting to them; he believes in the truth without thunder or trumpets and no more needs to associate God with tablets of stone or an ark than with a golden calf. He does not even need to feel that he must be righteous because he has been told of a great rewarder or eternal avenger. He is sufficiently admonished by his conscience and by reason. If he should be told, under pain of

eternal torment, that he must confess that three makes one, that a
man or a piece of bread are a god, he knows perfectly well what
to think of the threat but is careful not to laugh at the mystery
before he has studied its origin and has gathered its bearing. The
ignorance that denies strikes him as being just as rash as the
ignorance that affirms; but nothing ever surprises him, and where
obscure questions are concerned he is never quick to express an
opinion.

To escape the fascination of things there is no need to be
unmindful of their advantages and charms.

We follow the teachings of Homer in this matter. Odysseus
did not deprive himself of the pleasure of listening to the Sirens'
song; he simply took the most effective steps to ensure that this
pleasure neither delayed his voyage nor lured him onto the rocks.
He split Circe's cup and intimidated her with his sword, but he
did not deny himself her caresses – only he took them instead of
having to pay for them or yielding to her will. To destroy
religion because of the existence of dangerous superstitions
would be like eradicating the vine to escape the dangers of
drunkenness or abjuring the delights of love to avoid its
disappointments and excesses.

As already mentioned, dogma has two faces: one light, the
other dark; let us follow the light without trying to abolish the
dark, for shadow is necessary for the revelation of brightness.
Jesus said once that offences must needs be and perhaps, if we
were really pressed for an answer, we should have to say that
superstitions are necessary. It is impossible to overstress this truth
which is so disregarded nowadays, that even if all men must be
equal before the law, they are certainly not equal in intelligence
and will-power.

Dogma is the great universal epic of faith, hope and love; it is
the poetic expression of nations; it is the immortal flowering of
human genius. It must be cultivated and conserved entire. Not a
word must be lost, not a symbol, an enigma or an image
discarded. Take the case of a child who has been brought up on
La Fontaine's Fables and has taken it for granted until the age of
seven that ants can talk to grasshoppers, will he tear up or throw
on the fire the delightful book, given him by his mother, as soon
as he is intelligent enough to realize that anyone who says that
creatures devoid of reasoning ability can hold an intelligent

conversation is either mad or pretending?

Respect for authority has to be added to respect for dogma, that is to say respect for the hierarchy, to whom it is necessary to submit externally when it is only external and internally when it is a real priesthood. If society or the Church has given me as master a man who knows less than I do, I must keep silent before him and act according to my lights; but if he is wiser than I and better too, I must listen to him and profit by his advice.

To avoid being fascinated by men and women we must never give our whole heart to changeable and perishable individualities. Let us love the immortal virtues and eternal flower of beauty which we see in transient creatures. If our pet bird flies away let us not think badly of all birds; and if the roses we have cut, whose scent is such a joy, fade in our hands, let us not imagine that all the rose-bushes are dead and that spring has shed its blossoms. An individual rose dies very quickly, but the *rose* is eternal. Must a musician give up music because he has broken his violin? There are certain birds which are so constituted that they cannot survive the winter; they need an eternal spring and, for them alone, spring never ceases on earth. I am talking about the swallows, and you know what they do to obtain this miracle quite naturally. When the year has lost its prime they migrate to where the warm season is just beginning and when the spring is no longer where they are they go where the spring has gone.

CHAPTER XIV
Dark Intelligence

Those whom initiates are entitled to call profane, the vile multitude, that is to say the feeble masses perverse in mind and heart, those who adore a shadowy god or pay lip service to atheism (you know the type of people I mean) always listen without understanding, because they are presumptuous and unreliable. If a doctrine is presented to them in an absurd form to please them, they inevitably understand it in an even more absurd sense and often take it completely the wrong way.

Thus, when they repeat mechanically that there is one God in three Persons you will find, if you question them, that for them this means one Person in three Gods.

They have been told, and they repeat, that God, that is to say the fount of infinite goodness, is everywhere, but they concede that there are vast spaces of darkness where God is not, where eternal damnation, or deprivation of God, is suffered.

'What would you do' asked the theologian Tauler to a poor man or, rather, to a poverty-stricken man, because the poor man was the theologian himself, 'What would you do if God was intending to throw you into Hell?'

'I should take Him with me', answered the sublime pauper, 'and Hell would be turned into Heaven.'

Theologians may admire this reply but they will certainly not understand it.

'Yes,' some doctor of the law will say, 'God is in Hell, but only as an avenger.'

'Play the part of the executioner and we shall get rid of the Devil who is now redundant; that will be something gained anyway.'

When they talk about redemption, they mean that God, having consigned all His children to the Devil (for the very serious matter of an apple) in a fit of anger, has been obliged to suffer unending death to ransom them eternally and securely.

If you mention the Qabalah to them they invariably visualize it as a coded grimoire which is used to summon the Devil and to rule the fantasy world of sylphs, gnomes, salamanders and undines. If the conversation turns to magic, they think of it in terms of Circe's wand and enchanted cup which changes men into swine. They easily confuse Zoroaster with Muhammad and, as for Hermes Trismegistus, they think that that is some strange name used to mystify the ignorant, just as the word 'Bogy-man' is used to intimidate children.

Ignorance, like faith, has its orthodoxy; and if one happens to know things which are unknown to the so-called learned, one is a heretic in their eyes. Because there are no new truths, the wise men of this world support their authority on tottering error.

Besides, it is well known that accepted error props up almost every standpoint. 'How dare you answer the High Priest like that!' shouts an officer as he strikes Jesus who has spoken with respectful firmness. 'Are you trying to say, you nobody, that when the authorities accuse you they expose their own ignorance? Are you telling us that you know something unknown to the powers-that-be? So the High Priest is wrong is he, and you know he is wrong? He is talking nonsense and you are talking sense?'

Napoleon I detested ideologies because he himself was the world's leading ideologist. He wanted to carry all before him without resistance, but was unable to offer any resistance when the striking power he had deployed for so long was suddenly turned against him.

Since the dawn of history, we see that it is always the lie which has ruled the earth, while truth has asserted its rule from time to time in violent disasters and plagues. Cruel and inflexible Truth! Is it surprising that men do not like you? Time and again you destroy the illusions of kings and commoners and if, on occasions, you have your devoted servants, you abandon them and turn them over to the cross, the stake and the scaffold! Blessed are those who die for you, but wiser are those who serve you with sufficient adroitness to avoid a useless martyrdom. There is no doubt that Rabelais was a greater philosopher than Socrates, since by hiding behind the mask of Aristophanes he managed to escape the attentions of the breed of Anitus and Melitus (who are always with us).

Galileo, whose name in itself would make the Holy Inquisition a laughing-stock for all time, had sense enough not to brave the torture chamber and the dungeon. Contemporary documents show him as a prisoner in a palace drinking with the inquisitors and signing *inter pocula* (between drinks) his ironic deed of abjuration, far from saying with a stamp of his foot and a clenched fist, '*Eppur si muove*' ('It does move, all the same'). It is said that he added, 'Yes, I affirm on your word that the earth is immobile, and if you like I will add that the heavens are made of glass, and if it pleased God that your foreheads were the same they would let in the light'. Rabelais would have turned and said, 'Let's drink on that!'

Would it not be the most ridiculous form of suicide to die in order to prove to fools that two and two make four? A theorem which has been demonstrated cannot be denied, and the abjuration of a mathematical truth is nothing more than a farce and a grimace, the absurdity of which will attach itself to those who can seriously exact it in the name of an alleged infallible authority. If Galileo had gone to the stake for protesting against the Church, he would have been a heresiarch. By abjuring as a Catholic what he had demonstrated as a scientist, he killed the Catholicism of the Middle Ages.

One day someone handed the author of this book an article from the *Syllabus* saying, 'Take a look, here is the formal condemnation of your doctrines. If you are a Catholic, admit the charge and burn your books; if, on the other hand, you are going to persist in your teachings, don't let's hear any more about your catholicity.'

The article from the *Syllabus* is number seven in Section Two and the doctrines it condemns are these:

'The prophecy and miracles made known and recorded in Scripture are poetic fictions and the mysteries of the Christian faith are an epitome of philosophic investigations; contained in the books of the two Testaments are mystical inventions and Jesus Himself is a myth.'

What was the astonishment of the person who was trying to confound me when I said that these were no doctrines of mine. I said to him, 'Here is what I teach or, rather what is recognized by the Church, by science and by myself.'

'The narratives of the prophecies and miracles in the Bible have a poetic form which is peculiar to the oriental genius. The mysteries of the Christian faith have been confirmed and explained, as to their expression, by philosophic investigations. The Old and New Testaments contain parables and Jesus Himself has been the subject of many parables and legends.'

I fearlessly submit these propositions to the Pope and to the future Council, and am quite certain in advance that they will not condemn them.

What the Church does not want, and rightly so, is to be deliberately contradicted. Her infallibility is needed to maintain peace in the Christian world, so she must preserve her infallibility at all costs. If she were to say that two and two make three, I should take care not to say she was mistaken. I should endeavour to find how and in what manner two and two could make three, and you may be sure I would be successful. For example: two apples and two halves of an apple make three apples. When the Church seems to utter an absurdity, it is merely an enigma propounded to test the faith of the faithful.

Needless to say, it will be a grand and moving spectacle, this next General Council, when the queen of the Old World, wrapped in her tattered purple, declares that she is more sovereign than ever — at the moment she falls from her throne, and proclaims her extended rights and new pretensions in the face of imminent spoliation. The bishops will be as heroic as those sailors of the *Vengeur* who, on a ship ready to founder, were full of defiance instead of surrendering and fired their last broadside as they nailed their flag to the remaining stump of the mainmast.

Besides, they know that a compromise would utterly ruin them and that the altar flames would go out as soon as they ceased to be in darkness. When the temple veil is rent the gods depart, to return when new dogmatic embroidery makes a new veil lightproof.

Night is for ever backing away from the advance of day, but only to take possession of regions on the other side of the globe which the sun has abandoned. There is need of darkness, there is need of impenetrable mysteries to baffle that dark intelligence which believes in the absurd and combines the despotism of a limited reasoning power with the immeasurable audacity of faith. Daylight circumscribes our horizons and gives us a sight of the limits of the world; it is night, more than anything else, boundless night with its immense haze of stars, which gives rise to our sense of the infinite.

Study the child, he is man as he leaves the hands of nature, to use the language of Rousseau, and see the bent of his mind. Realities bore him, fictions excite him; he understands everything except for mathematics; he would rather believe fables than history. It is because the first period of life has a joyful infinity about it; it is because the future seems so marvellous in the initial stages of existence that it is natural to dream of giants and fairies in the middle of such miracles. It is because the poetic faculty, the divinest of human faculties, represents the world at first as a cloud in the sky. This sense is a sweet folly which is often wiser than reason, if I may so speak, because our reason always brings us face to face with narrow limits which science attempts to push back bit by bit, whereas poetry leaps into infinity with its eyes shut and strews there all the stars of our dreams.

The task of the Church is to keep the beliefs of a childish fancy within bounds. Fools are indisciplined believers and the faithful believers are fools who recognize the authority of that wisdom which is represented by the priesthood.

Let the priesthood only become a real priesthood and the leaders of the blind no longer blind themselves and the Church will save society by recovering her great virtues and her power.

Science itself requires the night in order to observe the multitude of stars. The sun conceals the stars from us; the night shows them to us, and they seem to flower in the dim sky like superhuman inspirations shining in the darkness of faith. Angels' wings look white during the night; by day they are black.

Dogma is not unreasonable, it is extra-reasonable or supra-reasonable and has always summarized the highest aspirations of occult philosophy. If you read the history of the councils you will always see a glimpse of progress and reason in the trends set by the great heretics. The Church always appears to affirm what is absurd and to come down on the side of the dark intelligence. Thus when Arius thought he was safeguarding the unity of God by imagining a substance analogous but superior to that of God (the substance of God, who is immaterial and infinite!), the

Church proclaimed at Nicaea a unity of substance analogous to the unity of God.

When an attempt was made to represent Jesus Christ as a hybrid personage composed of a divine person and a human person, the Church rejected this blend of the finite and the infinite and declared that there could only be one person in Jesus Christ. When Pelagius took an exaggerated view of human pride and the obligations of free will and consigned the mass of sinners irremediably to Hell, the Church affirmed that grace which works for the salvation of the unrighteous and makes up for human failure by the virtues of election. Pompous Protestants are indignant at the prerogatives accorded to the Virgin, Mother of God, and do not see that in this adorable personification, humanity has been snatched from the contamination of original sin and the act of generation has been rehabilitated. This woman who is extolled is a glorified mother: *Credo in unam, sanctam, catholicam et apostolicam Ecclesiam.* (I believe in one, holy, catholic and apostolic Church).

Catholic (that is to say 'universal') doctrine resembles the cloud which went before the children of Israel in the desert — obscure by day and bright by night. This doctrine is a stumbling block to false sages and the light of the ignorant. At the crossing of the Red Sea, the cloud stationed itself between the Hebrews and the Egyptians, according to Exodus. It shone on Israel and blotted out the light for the Egyptians. Thus has it always been for the universal dogma, which is only comprehensible to initiates. At one and the same time it is dark and clear. To do away with the shadow cast by the pyramids, the pyramids would have to be knocked down; the same is true of the obfuscations inherent in the eternal dogma.

It is said and repeated daily that no reconciliation is possible between religion and science. But people are using the wrong word: the one they should be using is not 'reconciliation' but 'fusion' or 'confusion'. If science and faith have so far appeared irreconcilable, it is due to the continual vain attempts to mix them together or to take one for the other. There is only one way of reconciling them and that is to distinguish between them and to separate them one from the other completely and absolutely. It would be just as ridiculous to ask the Pope how to demonstrate a theorem as it would be to ask a mathematician to settle a theological puzzle. The Immaculate Conception of the Virgin is not a question of embryology and the table of logarithms has nothing to do with the tables of the law. Science is compelled to admit whatever has been proved; and when faith is regulated by a reasonable authority, which it is also necessary to accept, it can reject nothing that is an article of faith.

Science will never demonstrate the existence of God or of the soul, and the Church has been forced to retract in the face of the proofs for Copernicus' and Galileo's systems of the universe. But does this signify that she can be deceived in matters of faith? No, all it means is that she must keep within her own jurisdiction. Even she does not claim that God has revealed to her the theorems of universal knowledge.

What science can observe are the phenomena produced by faith, and it can then, according to the saying of Jesus Christ Himself, judge the tree by its fruits. It is obvious that a belief which does not make men better, which does not elevate their thoughts, which does not strengthen their wills for goodness, beauty and justice alone, is an evil and perverted belief. The Judaism of Moses and the Bible made the grand nation of Solomon and the Maccabees. The Jewry of the Rabbis and the late Talmud has made sordid usurers who infect the ghetto.

Catholicism, too, has its corrupt Talmud, it is the insane hotchpotch of theologians and casuists, it is the jurisprudence of the inquisitors, it is the nauseating mysticism of the Capuchins and the sanctimonious. The enemies of Christianity and the impure gain a substantial and shameful advantage from these doctrines. It is against this that one must protest by all available means, and not against the majesty of the orthodox dogmas.

As far back as the first centuries, when religion was both protected and contaminated by the Empire, certain Christians who are now called saints by the Church put the desert between them and their places of worship. Maybe they loved the altars with all their heart, but they went to weep and pray far from them. The present writer is a Catholic of the desert.

However, there is nothing frightful about the Thebaid, and he has always preferred the Abbey of Thelema, founded by Rabelais, to the Hermitage of Saint Anthony. The human race no longer needs ascetics, it needs sages and workers to live with it and for it: that is the price of salvation in these days.

There is a white god and a black god in the Qabalah of Rabbi Simeon Ben Jochai. In nature there are 'white' men and 'black' men and in occult philosophy, too, we find a white intelligence and a black intelligence.

Before the study of light can be scientific, it must be possible to calculate the intensity and direction of shadow. The painters with the greatest technical ability are those with a knowledge of light and dark.

A good teacher must be able to put himself in the place of those who find learning hard.

The dark intelligence is the divination of the mysteries of the night, a sense of the reality of invisible forms.

It is belief in a dim possibility. It is a beam of light shining into a dream. At night, all creatures are unsighted except those which, like the owl, the cat and the lynx, have phosphorus in their eyes. During the night, the owl can devour those birds which are then defenceless; let us have lynx eyes to help us fight the owls, but let us refrain from setting fire to the forest on the pretext of giving the birds some light.

Let us have respect for the mysteries of darkness while keeping our lamp lit, and let us also know how to throw a veil around our lamp so as not to attract those insects which, during the night, love to drink human blood.

CHAPTER XV
The Great Arcanum

The great arcanum, the inexpressible arcanum, the dangerous arcanum, the incomprehensible arcanum may be definitively formulated thus:

The divinity of man.

It is inexpressible because as soon as one tries to put it into words it becomes a lie and the most monstrous lie of all.

In fact, man is not God. And yet the most audacious, the most obscure and at the same time the most splendid of religions asks us to worship the man-God.

Jesus Christ, whom she declares to be truly man, wholly man, finite man and a mortal man like us is at the same time completely God, and theology dares to talk in paradoxes. It speaks of worship addressed to the flesh, of the eternity of one who dies, of the impassibility of one who suffers, of the immensity of one who transfigures himself, of the finite taking the virtuality of the infinite, in a word of the God-man who offers to make all men God.

The serpent promised: *'Eritis sicut dii'* ('You will be as gods'). Jesus Christ, bruising the serpent's head under the charming foot of His Mother, dared to say: *'Eritis non sicut dii, non sicut Deus, sed eritis Deus!'* ('You will be not "as gods", not "as God", but you will be God!')

You will be God, for God is my Father, my Father and I are one and I intend that you and I shall be one: *'ut omnes unum sint sicut ego et pater unum sumus.'* ('That you all may be one as I and my Father are one').

I have grown old and grey poring over the least known and most formidable books on occultism; my hair has fallen out; my beard has grown as long as those of the desert fathers; I have sought and found the key to the symbols of Zoroaster; I have

entered the crypts of the Manes; I have come upon the secret of
Hermes unawares while neglecting to keep clear of a corner of
the veil which eternally conceals the great work; I know the
nature of that colossal sphinx which sinks slowly into the sand as
it contemplates the pyramids; I have penetrated the enigmas of
the Brahmins; I know what mysteries Simeon Ben Jochai buried
with him during twelve years in the desert; the lost clavicules of
Solomon have appeared to me resplendent with light and I have
read fluently in the books which Mephistopheles himself was
unable to translate for Faust.

Nevertheless, nowhere, neither in Persia, nor in India, nor
among the palimpsests of ancient Egypt, nor in the forbidden
grimoires salvaged from the bonfires of the Middle Ages, have I
found a book so profound, more revealing, more luminous in its
mysteries, more frightening in its splendid revelations, more sure
in its prophecies, more searching into the depths of man and the
immense shadow of God, more grand, more true, more simple,
more terrible and more sweet than the Gospel of Jesus Christ.

What book has been more read, more admired, more
slandered, more travestied, more glorified, more wrested and
more ignored than that one! It is like honey in the mouth of the
wise and like strong poison in the belly of the world. The
Revolution was organized to fight it. Proudhon writhed as he
tried to spew it out. It is as invincible as truth and as elusive as
error.

What a blasphemy it would be to Israel to say that God is a
man, and what folly it would be to you Christians! What an
abominable paradox it would be to say that man can make
himself God! Crucify the profaner of the arcanum, burn the
initiators, *Christianos ad leonem*! (Christians to the lions!)

The Christians made use of the lions and the entire world,
conquered by the martyr to the darkness of the great arcanum,
found itself groping like Oedipus before the solution of the final
problem, that of the man-God.

The man-God is a truth, the cry went up, but he must be as
unique on earth as he is in Heaven. The man-God, infallible,
almighty, is the pope; and at the bottom of this proclamation
which has been written and repeated under all forms, one can
read such names as Alexander Borgia.

The man-God is liberated man, the Reformation said next: and that cry, which people hoped they could stuff down the Protestants' throats, ended up as the roar of the Revolution. The terrible word of the enigma was pronounced, but it became more enigmatic than before.

'What is truth?' asked Pilate in condemning Jesus Christ.

'What is liberty?' ask our modern Pilates as they wash their hands in the blood of the nations.

Ask the revolutionaries from Mirabeau to Garibaldi what liberty is, and they will never reach agreement.

For Robespierre and Marat, it is a chopper adjusted at a certain level; for Garibaldi it is a red shirt and a sabre.

For ideologists it is a declaration of the rights of man.

But what man are we talking about?

Is the convict suppressed because society chains him up? Has a man rights because he is a man or only when he behaves himself?

For the profane masses, liberty is the absolute assertion of their rights; rights which always seem to involve restrictions and servitude. If liberty is simply the right to do good, it is being confused with duty and can hardly be distinguished from virtue.

Everything which the world has seen and tried up to now has failed to solve the problem posed by magic and by the Gospel: the great arcanum of the man-God.

The man-God has neither rights nor duties, he has knowledge, will and power.

He is more than free, he is a master. He does not issue orders, he causes to be done. He does not obey, for none can command him. That which others call duty, he terms his good pleasure. He does good because he wishes to do it and could do no other. He freely co-operates with everything that is just, and for him sacrifice is the luxury of a moral life and magnificence of soul. He is implacable towards evil because he is without hatred for the wicked. He looks on corrective punishment as a benefit and does not understand the meaning of vengeance.

Such is the man who has succeeded in reaching the central point of balance and one can, without blasphemy or folly, call him the man-God, because his soul is identified with the eternal principle of truth and justice.

The liberty of the perfect man is the divine law itself; it soars above all human laws and all the conventional obligations of the religious systems. The law is made for man, said Christ, and not man for the law. The Son of Man is Lord of the Sabbath; that is to say, the requirement to keep the Sabbath, imposed by Moses under pain of death, only binds man in so far as it is useful to him, for in the final analysis man is the sovereign master. 'All is permissible for me,' said Saint Paul, 'but not everything is expedient', by which he meant that we have the right to do anything which harms neither ourselves nor others and that our freedom is only restricted by the warnings of our conscience and our reason.

The wise man never has any scruples; he behaves with common sense and only does what he wants to do; so in his own sphere he can do everything and is blameless. *Qui natus est ex Deo non peccat* (He who is born of God does not sin), says Saint Paul, because his errors being involuntary, cannot be imputed to him.

It is towards this sovereign independence that the human soul must advance through the difficulties of progress. This is veritably the great arcanum of occultism, because it is thus that the mysterious promise of the serpent is realized: 'You will be as gods knowing good and evil.'

This is how the serpent of Eden is transfigured and becomes the serpent of brass to heal all the wounds of humanity. Jesus Christ Himself has been compared to this serpent by the Church fathers because, said they, He has taken the form of sin to change the abundance of iniquity into the superabundance of justice.

We have spoken plainly here and have revealed the truth without veils, and yet we are not afraid that anyone can rightly accuse us of being someone who makes rash disclosures. Those who ought not to understand these pages will not understand them; for to a sight which is too weak, truth, when shown in all its nakedness, appears veiled in its own light and concealed beneath its own brilliant splendour.

CHAPTER XVI
The Agony of Solomon

Faith is one of the powers of youth and doubt is a symptom of senility.

The young man who believes in nothing is like a misbegotten infant with wrinkles and grizzled locks.

When the spirit weakens, when the heart's fires burn low, then one mistrusts truth and love. When one's eyes grow dim, one imagines that the sun no longer shines, and even life itself becomes a matter of doubt as one feels in advance the cold approach of death.

Consider the children. How their eyes shine; what tremendous faith they have in light, in goodness, in the infallibility of their mother, in the pronouncements of their nurse! What a mythology their inventions are! With what personality they endow their toys and dolls! What paradise the way they look conveys! Dear, beautiful angels! The eyes of little children are God's mirrors upon earth. The youth believes in love: his time of life is that of the 'Song of Solomon.'

The mature man believes in wealth, in success and, on occasions, even in wisdom. The 'Proverbs of Solomon' are concerned with this period of maturity.

Then a man ceases to be amiable and proclaims the vanity of love. He is surfeited, and no longer gives credence to the pleasures of riches. He loses his taste for success because of the errors and abuses of glory. His enthusiasm is exhausted, his generosity is worn out. He becomes egotistical and defiant, until at last he doubts knowledge and wisdom too. So Solomon turns to write his melancholy book of 'Ecclesiastes.'

What was left in him of that young man who wrote: 'My beloved is an only one among beautiful women ... love is stronger than death ... and all a man's goods and his life as well would be no price to pay for a share of love.'?

Alas! now read this in 'Ecclesiastes'; 'I have found a man in a thousand, but not one outstanding woman. I have studied all the errors of men and have discovered that woman is more bitter than death. Her charms are the hunter's snare and her gentle arms are chains.' Solomon, you have grown old!

This prince surpassed in magnificence all the monarchs of the East. He built the Temple which was one of the wonders of the world, the destined centre of Asiatic civilization according to Jewish belief. His ships plied to and fro with those of Hiram, king of Tyre. The wealth of all nations flowed into Jerusalem. He was known as the wisest of men and held sway as the most powerful of kings. He was initiated into the science of the sanctuaries and gathered all this knowledge together in a vast encyclopaedia. His numerous marriages allied him with all the Eastern powers. He then thought himself to be the absolute master of the world and imagined that the time had come to effect a synthesis of all faiths. He wanted to surround the inaccessible centre where the abstract unity of Jehovah was worshipped with brilliant incarnations of the deity in many numbers and forms. He wanted to open up Israel to the arts and to make it permissible to create gods with the sculptor's chisel.

Jehovah's Temple was as unique as the sun and Solomon thought he would complete his universe by giving this sun a court of planets and satellites; so he had other temples erected on the mountains round about Jerusalem. God, manifested in the phenomenon of time, was worshipped there under the name of Saturn or Moloch. Solomon retained all the symbolism of this great image, merely suppressing the sacrifices of children and human victims. He inaugurated festivals of beauty around the altar of Venus or Astarte – festivals of beauty, youth and love, that triple smile of God which heartens and comforts the earth.

If he had succeeded, the glory and power of Jerusalem would have frustrated that of Rome and there would have been no reason for Christianity. Solomon would have become the Messiah promised to the Hebrews. But rabbinical fanaticism took alarm. The ancient sages who attended Bathsheba's son came under suspicion of apostasy. The young scribes and the rabble who were stirred up by the Levites managed to outwit the inexperienced Rehoboam, Solomon's son, and the old king realized with a shock one day that his heir would not carry on his work. Doubt entered his heart and with the doubt a profound despair. It was then that he wrote: 'I have carried out monumental works and I shall have to leave everything to an heir who will possibly be a fool. Everything done under the sun is vanity and everything seems to run round in a fatal circle; down here, the just is no happier than the unjust, and to devote oneself to study is an empty pursuit, because increased wisdom brings increased sorrow. A man dies like an animal and nobody knows whether man's spirit rises heavenward or if that of the animal falls to the earth. The man who is too wise becomes dazed and folk do not know whether he should be loved or hated. Let us live a day at a time and remember that God will judge us.'

'Woe,' he said on another occasion, while musing bitterly on his son, 'woe to the nation whose prince is only a child.'

These fits of infinite sadness of a great soul, isolated on its pinnacle of power, feeling cut off from earth yet unable to soar higher, are reminiscent of the lamentations of Job and the cry of Jesus on Calvary: '*Eli, Eli, lama sabachthani*'. ('My God, My God, why hast Thou forsaken me?')

Instead of creating a united world with Jerusalem as its centre, Solomon sensed that his own kingdom would be violently torn apart. The populace was agitated and looked for reforms which may have been promised for a long time; the Temple was finished and the exceptional taxes which had been levied for its construction, or for which its construction was a pretext, had not been reduced.

An agitator named Jeroboam formed a political party in the provinces. Rehoboam, who had become the blind instrument of the self-styled conservatives, made an almost public bonfire of his father's philosophic books, which vanished completely after Solomon's death, and the old master of spirits, forsaken by those he loved, resembled that king of Thule in the German ballad, who wept in silence into his cup and drank his wine mixed with tears. It was then that he execrated joy, saying: 'Why have you deceived me?' It was then that he exclaimed: 'It is better to enter the house of weeping than the house of rejoicing'. But why? He does not say. Centuries later, a wisdom which was greater than his, come to wipe away all tears, would say: 'Blessed are you who weep now, because the day will come when you shall laugh'. Thus it was laughter and happiness which Jesus came to promise mankind. The apostle Paul wrote to his converts, 'Rejoice evermore; *semper gaudite.*'

The wise man weeps when he is happy and smiles bravely when he suffers. The ancient Church fathers contended against an eighth deadly sin and named it melancholy.

It is said that Solomon knew the secret virtues of stones and the properties of plants, but there was one secret he did not know when he wrote 'Ecclesiastes', a secret of felicity and life, a secret which drives boredom away by perpetuating well-being and hope:

THE SECRET OF NOT GROWING OLD!

Is there such a secret? Are there men who never grow old? Is Flamel's elixir a reality? And must we perforce believe, like those who are over-fond of the marvellous, that the celebrated alchemist of the rue des Ecrivains has cheated death and is still living with his wife Pernelle under an assumed name in rich solitude in the New World?

No, we do not believe in the immortality of man upon earth. But we believe and know that man can keep himself from growing old.

We are obliged to die when we have lived a century or thereabouts; it is always time then for the soul to lay aside its vestment, which is no longer in fashion; it is time, not to die, for as we have already said we do not believe in death, but to aspire to a second birth and to begin a new life.

Yet, up to one's last breath, one may retain the simple joys of childhood, the poetic ecstasies of the young man, the enthusiams of maturity. Right to the end, one may intoxicate one's spirit with flowers, with beauty and with smiles; one may ceaselessly recapture the past and always recover what has been lost. A real eternity can be found in the fine dream of life.

'How can this be achieved?' you will surely ask me. Read attentively and meditate seriously on what I am going to tell you:

It is necessary to forget oneself and live only for others.

When Jesus said: 'If anyone wishes to follow me, let him deny himself, take up his cross and come after me,'' did He mean us to bury ourselves in some lonely spot, He, who always lived among men, who took up little children and blessed them, who restored fallen women, despising neither their show of affection nor their tears, who ate and drank with the outcasts of pharisaism (so much so that it was said of Him, 'This man is a glutton and a winebibber'), who tenderly loved Saint John and the family of Lazarus, who tolerated Saint Peter, healed the sick and fed the multitudes whose resources He multiplied in loving miracles? In what respect does this life resemble that of a Trappist or a Stylite, and how dared the author of a celebrated treatise which recommended isolation and concentration on oneself to call such a book *The Imitation of Jesus Christ*?

To live in others, with others and for others is the secret of love and of eternal life. It is also that of everlasting youth. 'If you do not become as little children' said the Master, 'you will not enter the Kingdom of Heaven'.

To love is to live in those whom one loves, it is to think their thoughts, fathom their desires, share their affections; the more one loves the more one's own life is enlarged. The man who loves is not alone and his existence is in many places at once; his name is family, fatherland, humanity. He talks baby talk and plays with the children, joins in the enthusiasms of youth, holds a rational discussion with the middle-aged and clasps the hand of the old.

Solomon had lost his feelings of love when he wrote 'Ecclesiastes' and the decrepitude of his heart had plunged him into blindness of spirit. This book is the agony of a sublime spirit which is being extinguished for lack of a supply of love. It is as sad as the solitary genius of Chateaubriand, as the poems of the nineteenth century. And yet, the nineteenth century produced Victor Hugo, who is the living proof* of the things I have just been propounding. This man, who was egotistical to begin with, was old in his youth, and then, when his hair turned white he embraced love and became young again. How he loves children! How he respires all the vigour and all the divine follies of youth! What a grand pantheism of love there is in his last poems! He has the universal faith of Goethe and the philosophical range of Spinoza. He is Rabelais and Shakespeare. — Victor Hugo, you are a great magician without knowing it and you have had more success in finding the secret of eternal life than poor Solomon!

---

* In 1868, when this was written. Victor Hugo 1802-1885.

CHAPTER XVII
The Magnetism of Good

It is said and repeated every day that good people are miserable in this world while the wicked prosper and are happy. This is a stupid and abominable lie.

This falsehood stems from the common mistake which confuses wealth with felicity; as if one could reasonably say that Tiberius, Caligula, Nero and Vitellius were happy. They were rich though, and even more than that they were the masters of the world; yet their hearts had no rest, their nights were sleepless and their conscience was scourged by the furies.

Does a pig become a man when we serve it truffles in a trough of gold?

Happiness is within ourselves not in our porringers, and Malfilâtre dying of hunger would have deserved his fate if he had wished he were a fattened hog.

Who is the happier out of Socrates and Trimalcion (that character in Petronius who is the caricature of Claudius)? Trimalcion would have died of indigestion if he had not been poisoned.

Good people sometimes suffer poverty and even misery, I do not deny this, but often it is their very poverty which preserves their integrity. Wealth might corrupt and destroy them. We must not imagine that the really good people are those who belong to the great mass of fools of only moderate courage and weak wills. Fools who obey the law out of fear or spinelessness, devotees who fear the Devil and poor devils who fear God. People like that are dumb cattle who are able to profit neither by gold and riches nor by want; but can one ever seriously pity the wise, the truly wise? Even when the wise man is ill-treated it is by those who envy him. At this point several of my readers will say, with an air of disappointment, 'You promised us magic and you have given us morals. Enough of philosophy, tell us now about occult forces.'Very well! Those of you who have read my books will know what the two serpents of the Caduceus signify. They are the two opposing currents of the universal magnetism. Thje serpent of creative and preserving light and the serpent of eternal fire which devours in order to regenerate.

The good are magnetized, vivified and preserved by the imperishable light, the wicked are burnt in the eternal fire.

There is a magnetic and sympathetic communion between children and the light; they all bathe in the same source of life; they are all happy in their common blessings.

Positive magnetism is a force which gathers things together, whereas negative magnetism is a dispersive force.

Light attracts life and fire carries destruction with it.

White magnetism is sympathy and black magnetism is aversion.

Good people love one another and wicked people hate one another because they know all about each other.

The magnetism of those who are good attracts to them all that is good for them and when it does not attract riches it is because wealth would not be good for them.

The heroes of ancient philosophy and of primitive Christianity, you will recall, embraced holy poverty as a strict guardian of their work and temperance.

But anyway, are men of good-will ever poor? Have they not an endless supply of magnificent things to give away? To be rich is to give; to give is to amass, and one's eternal inheritance is altogether composed of what one bestows on others.

There is really and truly an atmosphere of good, just as there is an atmosphere of evil. In the one a man breathes in eternal life, in the other eternal death.

The symbolic circle in the shape of the good serpent biting its tail, the pleroma of the Gnostics, the nimbus of the saints in the Golden Legend, is the magnetism of good.

Every saintly head emits rays of light and the rays interlace to form chains of armour.

The rays of grace are linked with rays of glory; the certainties of Heaven fecundate the good desires of Earth. The just who are dead have not left us, they live in us and by us, they inspire us with their thoughts and rejoice in ours. We live in Heaven with them and they fight on earth with us side by side; for we will solemnly repeat what we have said before, the symbolic Heaven, the Heaven which the various religions promise to the righteous is not an estate, but rather a state of souls. Heaven is eternal, generous harmony, and Hell, irremediable Hell, is the inevitable conflict of dastardly instincts.

Muhammad, following oriental style, presented his disciples with an allegory which has been taken for an absurd story, pretty much as Voltaire took the parables in the Bible.

There is, said he, a tree called Tuba so vast and outbranching that a horse starting at a gallop from the foot of the tree would have to go on galloping for a hundred years before emerging from its shade. The trunk of this tree is made of gold and its branches bear leaves which are talismans, cut from marvellous stones, which shower on the true believers all that their heart can desire. They have only to be touched to yield delicious food or splendid garments. This tree is invisible to the ungodly but it extends one of its branches into the house of every just man and each branch has the properties of the whole tree.

That allegorical tree is the magnetism of good. It is what the Christians call grace. It is what the symbolism of Genesis refers to as the tree of life. Muhammad had divined the secrets of the Science and spoke as an initiate when recounting the beauties and wonders of the tree of gold, the gigantic tree Tuba.

'It is not good for man to be alone' said the eternal Wisdom, and this statement is the expression of a law. Man is never alone, either in good or in evil. His existence and feelings are individual and collective at one and the same time.

Everything which men of genius discover or attract from the light shines out for the whole of humanity. Every worthy thing done by the righteous profits all the just and, at the same time, affords grace for repentance to the wicked. The heart of humanity has strings in all hearts.

Everything that is true is beautiful. The only vanity under the sun is error and falsehood. Even pain and death are beautiful, because they are the work which purifies and the transfiguration which delivers. The fleeting forms are true because they are manifestations of the power and beauty of the eternal. Love is true. Woman is holy and her conception is immaculate. True knowledge never deceives; reasonable faith is not an illusion. A cheerful, sympathetic laugh is an act of faith, hope and charity. To go in dread of God is to fail to recognize Him; it is only error which should be dreaded. A man may do anything he wants to do when all he wants to do is justice. He may even, if he so wishes, rush into wrongdoing but he will be dashed to pieces if he does. God reveals Himself to man, in man and by man. His true worship is Charity. Dogmas and rites alter and succeed one another; charity does not change and its power is eternal.

There is only one sole and veritable power on earth as there is in Heaven: it is that of goodness. The righteous are the only masters of the world. The world is in upheaval when they suffer. It is transformed when they die. The oppression of justice is the compression of a force far more terrible than that of high explosives. It is not the masses who raise revolutions, but the kings. The just person is inviolable, woe to him who would touch him! The Caesars have fallen to cinders, burnt by the blood of the martyrs. Whatever a righteous man wishes is approved by God. Whatever a righteous man writes, God signs, and it is an everlasting testament.

The great clue to the riddle of the sphinx is God in man and in nature. Those who separate man from God separate him from nature, because nature is full of God and recoils in horror from atheism. Those who separate man from nature are like sons who would honour their father by cutting off his head. God is the head of nature, so to speak, she would not exist without Him, He would not manifest Himself without her.

God is our Father, but nature is our mother. 'Honour thy father and they mother,' says the Ten Commandments, 'that thy days may be long in the land.' *Emmanuel*, God is with you: this is the sacred word of the initiates who go only by the name of Brothers of the Rosy Cross (Rosicrucians). It is in this sense that Jesus Christ could call Himself the Son of God, and God Himself, without blasphemy. It is in this sense that He wants us only to make one with Him as He only makes one with His Father, so that regenerated humanity will realize in this world the great arcanum of the man-God.

Let us love God in one another, for God will never show Himself to us except in one another. Everything lovable about us comes from God in us. God is all there is to be loved, and it is only God whom one loves when one knows how to love truly.

God is light. He does not love darkness. Therefore, if we long to feel God within us, we must let the light into our souls. The tree of Knowledge is not a tree of death except for Satan and his apostles. *To the superstitious it is the Manchineel tree*, but to us it is the tree of life.*

Then we shall no longer say, like stupid slaves, 'This is good because we have been ordered to do it and have been promised a reward and that is bad because we have been told not to do it on pain of chastisement', but we shall say, 'Let us do this because we know that it is good and refrain from doing that because we know that it is evil.'

And thus will be realized the promise of the symbolic serpent: *'You will be as gods, knowing good and evil.'*

---

* The Manchineel tree is a tropical American tree with a poisonous and caustic milky sap.